Polydox Reflections

Directions in Modern Theology Book Series

Born out of the journal *Modern Theology*, the Directions in Modern Theology book series provides issues focused on important theological topics and texts in current debate within that discipline, whilst looking at broader contemporary topics from a theological perspective. It analyses notions and thinkers, as well as examining a wide spectrum of 'modern' theological eras: from late Medieval through to the Enlightenment and up until the present 'post-modern' movements. Attracting distinguished theologians from a world-wide base, the book series develops what is a unique forum for international debate on theological concerns.

Titles in the series include:

Heaven on Earth? Theological Interpretation in Ecumenical Dialogue
Edited by Hans Boersma and Matthew Levering

Faith, Rationality and the Passions
Edited by Sarah Coakley

Re-thinking Dionysius the Areopagite
Edited by Sarah Coakley and Charles M. Stang

The Promise of Scriptural Reasoning
Edited by David Ford and C. C. Pecknold

Aquinas in Dialogue: Thomas for the Twenty-First Century
Edited by Jim Fodor and Frederick Christian Bauerschmidt

Re-thinking Gregory of Nyssa
Edited by Sarah Coakley

Theology and Eschatology at the Turn of the Millennium
Edited by L. Gregory Jones and James Buckley

Catholicism and Catholicity: Eucharistic Communities in Historical and Contemporary Perspectives
Edited by Sarah Beckwith, L. Gregory Jones and James J. Buckley

Theology and Scriptural Imagination: Directions in Modern Theology
Edited by L. Gregory Jones and James Buckley

Spirituality and Social Embodiment
Edited by L. Gregory Jones and James Buckley

Polydox Reflections

Edited by

Mary-Jane Rubenstein and Kathryn Tanner

WILEY Blackwell

Published as Volume 30, Issue 3 of *Modern Theology*
© 2014 John Wiley & Sons Ltd

Blackwell Publishing was acquired by John Wiley & Sons in February 2007. Blackwell's publishing program has been merged with Wiley's global Scientific, Technical, and Medical business to form Wiley-Blackwell.

Registered Office
John Wiley & Sons Ltd, The Atrium, Southern Gate, Chichester, West Sussex, PO19 8SQ, UK

Editorial Offices
350 Main Street, Malden, MA 02148-5020, USA
9600 Garsington Road, Oxford, OX4 2DQ, UK
The Atrium, Southern Gate, Chichester, West Sussex, PO19 8SQ, UK

For details of our global editorial offices, for customer services, and for information about how to apply for permission to reuse the copyright material in this book please see our website at www.wiley.com/wiley-blackwell.

Library of Congress Cataloging-in-Publication Data has been applied for.

ISBN 9781118807149
ISSN 0266 7177 (Print)
ISSN 1468 0025 (Online)

A catalogue record for this book is available from the British Library.

Cover design by Richard Boxall Design Associates.

Set in 10 on 12 pt Palantino by Toppan Best-set Premedia Limited

Printed in Singapore.

1   2014

Modern Theology

Volume 30 No. 3   July 2014

CONTENTS

Special issue
"Polydox Reflections"
Guest Editors: Mary-Jane Rubenstein and Kathryn Tanner

Articles

Modern Theology 30:3 July 2014
ISSN 0266-7177 (Print)
ISSN 1468-0025 (Online)

DOI: 10.1111/moth.12117

INTRODUCING POLYDOXY

MARY-JANE RUBENSTEIN

This special issue of *Modern Theology* stages a critical conversation around the multivocal texts composing *Polydoxy: Theology of Multiplicity and Relation*, edited by Catherine Keller and Laurel Schneider.[1] That volume is in part the product of a Transdisciplinary Theological Colloquium at Drew University entitled, "Polydoxy: Theologies of the Manifold." In order to introduce, expand, and refine this vibrant set of theological possibilities, it is our hope in this issue to bring a diversity of perspectives to bear on some of the positions enacted in and as "polydoxy."

The participants in the conference and contributors to the volume are not members of anything like a "school" of polydoxy, nor do they all share any particular tradition or methodology. Rather, their very different backgrounds and projects operate out of what Keller and Schneider call a "triune intuition" to *multiplicity, unknowing*, and *relation*.[2] "Polydoxy," then, functions as a provisional name—a strategic and perhaps evanescent heading under which to assemble scholars whose theological sensibilities exhibit a striking inter-resonance. It is, in other words, more of a descriptive than a prescriptive term, and a loose one at that. Nevertheless, this tenuous assembly of thinkers does hope in naming their alliance to advance one another's constructive theological and ethical visions—in particular, their shared commitments to social, political, economic, racial, sexual, and environmental justice, which arise from and strengthen their multiple relational ontologies.

Perhaps fittingly, the name "polydoxy" is itself overdetermined. *Doxa* can, of course, mean "opinion"—as in the "right opinion" of ortho-doxy—but it can also mean "appearance," "illusion," "glory" and "praise." Gathered under this neologism are therefore a multiplicity of opinions, visions, and articulations of divine and created multiplicities from perspectives within,

Mary-Jane Rubenstein
Department of Religion, Wesleyan University, 171 Church Street, Middletown, CT 06459, USA
Email: mrubenstein@wesleyan.edu
 [1] Catherine Keller and Laurel Schneider, (eds), *Polydoxy: Theology of Multiplicity and Relation* (New York: Routledge, 2011).
 [2] Ibid., 1.

beyond, and at the unsteady boundaries of numerous Christian traditions. Attending to multiplicity by means of multiplicity, these authors hope among other things to unsettle an imperial theology's long-standing obsession with what Laurel Schneider has called "the logic of the One,"[3] and to transform a traditional object of onto-epistemological denigration—"*multiplicity itself*"— into "theology's resource".[4] But what is "multiplicity itself"?

For the most part, the editors and authors of *Polydoxy* use the term "multiplicity" in conscious distinction to "plurality." They suggest that if plurality names a profusion of discrete individuals, the *pli* of multiplicity encodes an "enfolded and unfolding relationality" among singularities that are constituted (and undone) precisely by means of these shifting relations.[5] Multiplicity, in other words, names tenuously *connected* differences—neither manyness nor oneness as such but rather "events of becoming folded together, intersecting, entangled as multiples".[6] To celebrate multiplicity as the very stuff of theology is therefore to attend to the stunning and fragile biodiversity of creation; the racial, gendered, and embodied multiplicities that constitute "humanity"; and perhaps most specifically to theology, the varieties of human wisdom through and in distinction to which Christian theologies and ecclesiologies have emerged. By extension, it is also to reflect upon the source of these multiplicities as itself multiple—on the manyoneness of a creator intimately bound up with the manifold of creation. And as it turns out, this may be the point of greatest doctrinal diversity among polydox thinkers. For some, God stands eternally above, beyond, and/or beneath the universe that God nevertheless suffuses. For others, God Godself *becomes* in inexorable relation to created relationalities. There are, in other words, numerous and even conflicting degrees of panentheism enacted in these pieces, and yet each theological vision acknowledges itself as the contingent product of specific, human, and therefore limited texts and contexts, and stands self-consciously subject to revision.

Hence the polydoxic significance of *unknowing* in the midst of multiplicity and relation. In line with the apophatic strands of Abrahamic and non-Abrahamic theologies alike (and bearing in mind the playful inessentiality of its own "name"), "polydoxy presumes a mindful uncertainty."[7] It remains open, responsive to new insights and earthly unfoldings, and mindful above all of the violence—colonial, imperial, psychological, corporeal—that accompanies and enacts absolute claims to a single truth. And it maintains this apophatic openness in complex relation to a teacher infamously subjected to such violence, as well as a church that so often reenacts it.

---

[3] Laurel Schneider, *Beyond Monotheism: A Theology of Multiplicity* (New York: Routledge, 2008).

[4] Keller and Schneider, *Polydoxy*, 1.

[5] Ibid., 7.

[6] Ibid.

[7] Ibid., 8.

Polydoxy therefore operates in complex relation to orthodoxy. It would be tempting to reduce this relationship to one of simple opposition—to say, for example, that in the face of orthodoxy's oneness, certainty, and autonomy, polydoxy unleashes manyness, uncertainty, and relation. But of course, these polydox values emerge from many of the sources (kataphatic, apophatic, and Trinitarian) that compose the orthodox tradition as such. So just as "multiplicity" names not an opposition to oneness but rather a difference both beyond and within oneness, polydoxy claims not an opposition to orthodoxy but a complex "intra-activity" with it.[8] This intra-activity expresses itself in numerous ways. In some deployments, "polydoxy" amounts to a kind of immanent critique of the distinction between orthodoxy and heresy—an exposition of the processes by which "rightness" establishes itself by disavowing, punishing, ridiculing, and/or annihilating whatever differs from it. In this way, heterodoxy can be shown to be constitutive of orthodoxy as such, as its repressed other(s).

Even setting to one side the production of heresy, however, polydoxy aims to reveal the extent to which orthodoxy is not the monolith to which many of its proponents and opponents tend to reduce it. Rather, beginning from the plural "beginning" of four canonical gospels (and a host of excluded others), emerging from the religio-cultural complexity of the ancient near eastern world, and unfolding through an often divergent multitude of councils, doctors, and fathers, orthodoxy *itself* is "always already polydox."[9] It is therefore the task of polydoxy to expose these constitutive multiplicities and to offer them back as renewed resources for theological action and rumination.

Polydox Reflections aims to explore, refine, and build upon some of polydoxy's openings, tactics, and concerns. Breaking with a common pattern, the plan for this special issue of *Modern Theology* was not to solicit review articles of the book, but rather to approach theologians and historians who might be "fellow travelers" with polydoxy—that is to say, broadly sympathetic, but also possibly skeptical and even critical of it. We therefore invited these authors to respond creatively to the book in light of their own theological sensibilities and projects. We asked them to explore polydoxy in light of their own sense of the task of modern theology, and perhaps to offer correctives or directives for future polydox trajectories. In short, the authors gathered here were asked to "think with" the book, rather than about it, in order not only to introduce it to a wide theological audience, but also to develop their own work and polydoxy "itself" in relation to one another.

The issue's first two essays establish the contours and stakes of polydoxy's relationship to orthodoxy. Engaging the fraught history of reciprocal constitutions of orthodoxy and heresy, Virginia Burrus cautions that if polydoxy

---

[8] I have borrowed this term from Karen Barad, *Meeting the Universe Halfway: Quantum Physics and the Entanglement of Matter and Meaning* (Durham, NC: Duke University Press, 2007).

[9] Keller and Schneider, *Polydoxy*, 7.

establishes itself in opposition to orthodoxy, it risks reduplicating the very operations of power it critiques. A crucial way to avoid such mimicry would be to resist essentializing "orthodoxy" by subjecting its "shifting constructions" to "critical historical investigation."[10] Offering this intervention, Burrus can be seen as both cautioning and advancing polydox thinking; in fact, a particularly polydox vision emerges in her constructive image of "theological generativity" as neither static nor linear but rather "rhizomatic," so that doctrine looks "less like a sapling than a bed of irises—or a field of crabgrass—neither one nor many, but always already a multiplicity."[11]

With Burrus, Shannon Craigo-Snell worries that even through polydox texts "resist a strict binary opposition between polydoxy and orthodoxy," they "functionally" reinscribe them "to a single epistemological viewpoint . . . the logic of the One."[12] Mobilizing Luce Irigaray's critical retelling of the allegory of the cave, Craigo-Snell concedes that the western epistemic insistence on oneness enacts gendered, racial, colonial, and ecological violence. Yet she reminds us that this particular vision of enlightenment is not the only way to understand Christian truth. Triangulating the seventeenth century fiery revelations of René Descartes, George Fox, and Blaise Pascal, Craigo-Snell unearths the remarkably flexible and highly contextual constitution of orthodoxy itself. This too, then, can be heard either as a critique of polydoxy or as a call for it to be more fully itself; that is, to attend to the specific ways in which orthodoxy is "always already polydox."[13]

If Burrus and Craigo-Snell push the limits of our understanding of orthodoxy, Clayton Crockett dives straight into heresy. In line with the etymology of *haireseis*, Crockett admits that "to insist on choice is to flirt with heresy," and then chooses to fold together three nontheistic theologies that lie at the edges or well beyond the fray of Christian traditions.[14] Tuning into Colleen Hartung's Derridean suggestion that "theology does not have to assume a God or divinity to be theological,"[15] Crockett hears nontheistic theological resonances in Hyo-dong Lee's neo-Confucian meditation on the Great Ultimate, a "unified multiplicity" which Crockett complicates further in relation to the Dao that cannot be named.[16] In all three of these trajectories, Crockett traces apophasis along a familiar razor's edge between faith and faithlessness, purification and blasphemy, panentheism and atheism. Multiplicity, then, is

---

[10] Burrus, p. 9 internal reference.
[11] Burrus, p. 11 internal reference.
[12] Craigo-Snell, p. 18 internal reference.
[13] Keller and Schneider, *Polydoxy*, 2.
[14] Crockett, p. 34 internal reference.
[15] Coleen Hartung, "Faith and polydoxy in the whirlwind," in Keller and Schneider, *Polydoxy*, 153.
[16] Hyo-dong Lee, " 'Empty and tranquil, and yet all things are already luxuriantly present': a comparative theological reflection on the manifold Spirit," in Keller and Schneider, *Polydoxy*, 128 and Crockett, p. 42 internal reference.

internal not only to orthodoxy, but also to the heresy it calls forth and repudiates. In fact, heresy often looks a lot like orthodoxy—especially at the misty peaks of apophasis.

It is these peaks, which one could also configure as an abyss, that Linn Tonstad inhabits "as a queer and feminist theologian with a dogmatic orientation."[17] Maintaining what she calls a "polyfidelity" to what are usually marked as wildly "divergent discourses," Tonstad investigates a common systematic response to feminist, queer, and postcolonial critics of Trinitarian formulations.[18] In response to the charge that the name "Father" is a human projection that reinscribes oppressive systems of sex and gender, many systematic theologians insist that divine fatherhood is utterly different from human fatherhood, and therefore untainted by the patriarchal accretions of ordinary uses of the term. After demonstrating the inevitable collapse of these efforts, Tonstad asks in surprising solidarity with Crockett what it would mean for systematic theology "to speak 'Father' without fatherhood."[19] Ultimately, she suggests, such an effort would require abandoning the singularity of theological method and object alike, deploying "polyfidelity" to mirror the irreducible polydivinity of the Trinity.

Offering a different vision from and of the mist, Graham Ward responds to the polydoxic "gift" through a bifocal scriptural lens. To examine "the roles of revealed truth and authority within polydoxy's project,"[20] Ward trains half of our vision on James's likening life in Christ to "a mist that appears for a time and then vanishes" (James 4:14) and the other half on Jesus's parting words: "no longer do I call you servants . . . but I have called you friends" (John 15:15). Like Burrus's (Deleuzian) rhizome, the Jamesian mist becomes Ward's generous offering to the polydox project, hovering as it does in a plurisingularity poised "between a fading in and a fading out."[21] This mutable, unified manyness enacts for Ward the logic of Ephesians, whose "one," multiply and differently iterated, "does not mean homogeneity."[22] The essay concludes by posing two interrelated questions: the first concerning the nature of polydox Christology and the second concerning the value of multiplicity itself—in particular, the danger of affirming *everything* in affirming multiplicity, including the "depths of hatred, anguish, fear and impotence all around and within us."[23] How, he seems to ask, can polydoxy claim multiplicity as a theological resource if multiplicity contains the very violent formations polydoxy seeks to unsettle? And what does any of this have to do with Christology?

---

[17] Tonstad, p. 51 internal reference.
[18] Tonstad, p. 54 internal reference.
[19] Tonstad, p. 72 internal reference.
[20] Ward, p. 76 internal reference.
[21] Ward, p. 77 internal reference.
[22] Ward, p. 78 internal reference.
[23] Ward, p. 88 internal reference.

While other authors might address these questions differently, Mark Jordan's and Wendy Farley's reflections each offer compellingly polydox gestures toward a response. Mark Jordan performs his engagement of polydoxy—in particular, its attunement to *method*—through a series of inter-related fragments. In relation to Mayra Rivera's essay on the doxological polyvalence of "glory," Jordan asks what it means to "write theology" in the face of empire, which is to say in the face of terrorized and tortured human bodies.[24] Reminding us of Christianity's complicity with modern torture on the one hand, and of its commemoration of a tortured savior on the other, Jordan revisits some of Michel Foucault's literary essays to ask how we might live and write in relation to that ambivalent history—that is, how to com-memorate an act of violence liturgically, personally, and communally without sensationalizing or romanticizing the story—or worse, re-enacting it against others. For Jordan, such living and writing would emerge not in disavowing "the imperial terrors that theology can authorize," but rather in facing them courageously, hoping against hope that a new, transformative God-speech might emerge within the neglected interstices of empire.[25]

In Wendy Farley's essay, Jordan's meditation on the tortured rabbi and a tortured humanity is extended out to the tortured earth itself—to the raided forests, parched soil, dying oceans, disappearing species, endless wars, and innumerable oppressions of human and nonhuman animals that demand a wholesale reorientation of our theo-political worldview. Joining her voice to those polydox and even neo-orthodox critics of post-Constantinian ortho-doxy, Farley recounts the excruciating history of coercion, discipline, torture, war, "re-education," and repression stemming from the "mind-boggling stu-pidity of authoritarian regimes of knowledge."[26] As an antidote, she offers not so much a counter-theology as a corrective spirituality—drawn both from Christian and non-Christian sources.[27]

In their introduction to *Polydoxy*, Keller and Schneider write that although the volume tends to shy away from doctrinal certainties, it does make one specific "doctrinal claim . . . about what it means to be a Christian in this world. It requires a receptive posture toward a manifold of texts within and beyond the corpus of interpretations, practices, and spiritualities of those who claim the tradition/s of Jesus."[28] In attending to a small portion of this manifold, it is our hope that the present collections of essays will serve not only as an introduction to the stakes and methodologies of polydoxy, but as part of its continual unfolding: self-critical, provisional, rhizo-misty, *open*.

---

[24] Jordan, p. 100 internal reference and Mayra Rivera, "Glory: the first passion of theology?" in Keller and Schneider, *Polydoxy*, 167–185.
[25] Jordan, p. 104 internal reference.
[26] Farley, p. 115 internal reference.
[27] Ibid.
[28] Keller and Schneider, *Polydoxy*, 5.

Modern Theology 30:3 July 2014
ISSN 0266-7177 (Print)
ISSN 1468-0025 (Online)

DOI: 10.1111/moth.12118

HISTORY, THEOLOGY, ORTHODOXY, POLYDOXY

VIRGINIA BURRUS

Orthodoxy Versus Heresy

For historians of Christianity who are interested in thinking outside the Eusebian box, orthodoxy presents an enormous challenge, as Walter Bauer has long since argued—and also, alas, inadvertently demonstrated via his own failure to escape the constraints of the very categories he so astutely criticized.[1] Bauer's interrogation of the Eusebian view that orthodoxy represents a pure and originary Christianity, with heresy its later corruption, has survived the test of time where his reconstructions of earliest Christian history for the most part have not. As many have observed, Bauer's history remains trapped by its own defiant strategy of inversion, which leaves the categories of orthodoxy and heresy (or alternately heterodoxy) intact, even as it provocatively reverses traditional chronologies and hierarchies of valorization: "orthodoxy" emerges later than "heresies" and is marked by the will to dominate and suppress.[2] Post-Bauer, it has become conventional to give at least a polite nod to the "diversity" of ancient Christianity. What historians of ancient Christianity are still largely lacking, however—what Bauer failed to deliver—is a new model to replace the old binary, a model that can accommodate greater complexities of difference articulated within shifting fields of discourse and power.

Virginia Burrus
Department of Religion, Syracuse University, 501 Hall of Languages, Syracuse, NY 13244, USA
Email: mvburrus@syr.edu

[1] Walter Bauer, *Orthodoxy and Heresy in Earliest Christianity* (Philadelphia, PA: Fortress Press, 1971; German original, 1934).

[2] See, for example, Lewis Ayres's comments in "The Question of Orthodoxy," *Journal of Early Christian Studies*, Vol. 14, no. 4 (Winter, 2006): 395–398, as well as the translation of Walther Völker's 1935 review that appears in the same volume, "Walther Bauer's *Rechtgläubigkeit und Ketzerei im Ältesten Christentum*," translated by Thomas P. Scheck, 399–405.

Alain Le Boulluec has taken us much farther toward this goal by identifying orthodoxy and heresy as twinned discursive constructions—not fixed essences that exist prior to or independently of discourse but mobile concepts initially forged in second-century struggles for identity that swiftly become central to Christian self-definition in communities across the Mediterranean.[3] The discourse of orthodoxy does not, then, simply name pre-established differences but rather attempts to impose clarifying doctrinal distinctions and simplifying relations of power on diverse historical contexts typically characterized by enormous complexity and ambiguity—socially, culturally, and theologically. As Rebecca Lyman has argued, adding an explicitly post-colonial twist to LeBoulluec's implicitly Foucaultian analysis, the rhetoric of orthodoxy participates in broader Hellenistic discourses of universalism articulated within an intensely pluralistic, competitive, and mobile society charged by the pressures (and oppressions) of empire and colonialism.[4] Daniel Boyarin has further highlighted the particular place of heresiological discourse in the mutual, if unsteady, articulation of Jewish-Christian difference in this same period and context.[5]

Pre-Constantinian orthodoxy thus provides a window opening from the margins onto wider cultural negotiations of unity and multiplicity, sameness and difference, in the early Roman imperial period. Eventually, with the rise of an imperially patronized church and the evolution of a more effectively institutionalized apparatus of orthodoxy, Christianity overtakes the center and begins to set the terms of these cultural negotiations, both reflecting and shaping the contours of a public discourse framed by an imperial autocracy that now, more than ever before, enshrines the unity of "consensus" while simultaneously problematizing differences that are, paradoxically, thereby rendered more visible than ever.[6] However consistent the appeals to orthodoxy on the part of late ancient Christians, the very flexibility of the discourse that facilitates its hegemony also renders it extremely unstable—as anyone even slightly familiar with the history of theological controversy in the later

---

[3] Alain Le Boulluec, *La notion d'hérésie dans la littérature grecque IIe-IIIe siècles* (Paris: Études augustiniennes, 1985).

[4] Rebecca Lyman, "Hellenism and Heresy," *Journal of Early Christian Studies*, Vol. 11, no. 2 (Summer, 2003): 209–22, and "The Politics of Passing: Justin Martyr's Conversion as a Problem of 'Hellenization,' " in *Conversion in Late Antiquity and the Early Middle Ages: Seeing and Believing*, eds. Kenneth Mills and Anthony Grafton (Rochester, NY: University of Rochester Press, 2003), 36–60.

[5] Daniel Boyarin, *Border Lines: The Partition of Judaeo-Christianity*, Divinations: Rereading Late Ancient Religion (Philadelphia, PA: University of Pennsylvania Press, 2004).

[6] The relevant bibliography is by now extensive, and I will not attempt to provide a comprehensive list. My own *The Making of a Heretic: Gender, Authority, and the Priscillianist Controversy*, The Transformation of the Classical Heritage (Berkeley, CA: University of California Press, 1995), represents a localized attempt to give an account of the apparatus of orthodoxy as it emerges in the late fourth century. Many of the essays in Susanna Elm, Eric Rebillard, and Antonella Romano, eds., *Orthodoxie, Christianisme, Histoire: Orthodoxy, Christianity, Heresy* (Rome: École française de Rome, 2000) are also directly relevant.

Roman empire is aware. The doctrinal creeds of late antiquity, limned by corresponding anathematizations of those teachings and teachers deemed heretical, are the tenuous products of hard-won compromises reached through conciliar negotiation and underwritten by imperial power. To the extent that the authority of such creeds and anathemas is sustained (and of course it is not always sustained), this occurs through ongoing historical processes of renegotiation and reinterpretation, as the tacit toleration of difference alternates with forceful repressions of dissent.

If history itself does not yield a stable definition of orthodoxy, then orthodoxy should no longer order our church histories uncritically, as it ordered Eusebius's history and those of so many of Eusebius's successors, down to the present textbooks generally available for classroom use. Rather, the shifting constructions of orthodoxy must themselves be subjected to critical historical investigation. The documents of ancient Christianity reveal subtleties of differentiation and diversity that only sometimes come to be framed in polarized terms, as well as violent simplifications of asserted polarities that inevitably hide as much as they reveal about the textured fabric of a religious movement that placed nearly unprecedented value on both unity and universality even as it thereby also embraced the formidable difficulties entailed by an extreme social, cultural, and theological pluralism. Our histories will depart from Eusebius not by acknowledging diversity—for Eusebius too acknowledges diversity—but by refusing to harness the historical analysis of Christian difference to the narrow purposes of theological apologetics. Our histories will not thereby simply become more neutral or less engaged, however. They will, on the contrary, become accountable to a wider range of possible interests.

Development Versus Corruption

Orthodoxy presents an enormous challenge not only to historians but also to theologians. While it is among the peculiar characteristics of church history that it has frequently been overshadowed by particular theological interests, it is also among the peculiar characteristics of theology that it is ever haunted by the ghosts of the past. To theologize *de novo* or *ex nihilo* is simply not possible: even mystics typically articulate their most startling revelations within a dense intertextual web of theological tradition. Despite the inevitable transience and mutability of theological discourse, there remains a privileged "relation between Christian doctrine today and its earlier manifestations," as Maurice Wiles puts it—"the sense of a special relationship to the past."[7] At this point, the problematic of heresy emerges less as the product of the Eusebian binary critiqued by Walter Bauer than as the side-effect of the developmental model advanced by John Henry Newman and persistently

---

[7] Maurice Wiles, *The Remaking of Christian Doctrine* (London: SCM Press Ltd., 1974), 2, 9.

interrogated by Wiles:[8] if orthodoxy reflects the continuous and enduring development of the seed of apostolic faith, argues Newman, heresy is a deviant, discontinuous and short-lived growth.[9] Yet the binary and developmental models are scarcely unrelated. Doctrinal developmentalism renders apostolic tradition a somewhat less static phenomenon—indeed, it assumes doctrine's historical evolution to be an evident fact—but it continues to distinguish authoritatively between a single trajectory of authentic development and the many corruptions or perversions of truth.

As Wiles among others has argued, what is missing in Newman's account is not merely an adequate criterion for identifying an authentic development (Newman's seven "tests" notwithstanding)[10] but also an adequate model for conceptualizing the complexity of the historical process of doctrinal production. If the analogy of the seed favored by Newman suggests the singularity and linearity assumed by the developmental model ("germination, growth, and perfection"),[11] the analogy of the rhizome might offer an alternate botanical model for interpreting theological generativity. Rhizomatic reproduction occurs within a decentered, horizontal network of underground stems that strike new roots downwards and shoot new stems upward out of dispersed nodes. As Gilles Deleuze and Felix Guattari point out, "any point of a rhizome can be connected to any other, and must be. This is very different from the tree or root, which plots a point, fixes an order." Applying the concept of the rhizome to semiotic theory, they continue:

There is no mother tongue, only a power takeover by a dominant language within a political multiplicity. Language stabilizes around a parish, a bishopric, a capital. It forms a bulb. It evolves by subterranean stems and flows, along river valleys or train tracks; it spreads like a patch of oil. It is always possible to break a language down into internal structural elements, an undertaking not fundamentally different from a search for roots. There is always something genealogical about a tree. It is not a method for the people. A method of the rhizome type, on the contrary, can analyze language only by decentering it onto other dimensions and

---

[8] See especially Maurice Wiles, *The Making of Christian Doctrine* (Cambridge: Cambridge University Press, 1967) and Wiles, *The Remaking of Christian Doctrine*.
[9] The classic text is, of course, John Henry Cardinal Newman, *An Essay on the Development of Christian Doctrine*. I have here made use of the first edition of 1845, reissued by Penguin Books in 1974: *An Essay on the Development of Christian Doctrine: The Edition of 1845*, edited and with introduction by J. M. Cameron (Middlesex, England: Penguin Books, 1974). For an examination of the intellectual context of Newman's understanding of development, see Owen Chadwick, *From Bossuet to Newman*, second edition (Cambridge: Cambridge University Press, 1987).
[10] These are: preservation of type or idea; continuity of principles; power of assimilation; early anticipation; logical sequence; preservative additions; and chronic continuance (Newman, *Essay*, 116–47).
[11] Ibid., 99.

other registers. A language is never closed upon itself, except as a function of impotence.[12]

If, as I have suggested, a historical investigation of orthodoxy reveals that it is not only a remarkably persistent and flexible but also a remarkably unstable and mutable phenomenon, then a theological discourse that takes seriously its historicity also opens itself to instability and unpredictability, and hence to the dynamism of its own generative *multiplicity*. However we may understand the elusive initiating moment in Jesus Christ, the historical record suggests that Christian teaching spread both rapidly and in multiple directions; moreover, despite the irreducible differences of its regional inflections as well as frequent eruptions of conflict, this teaching seems to have displayed a consistent sense of its own connectivity.[13] Doctrine emerges, then, looking less like a sapling than a bed of irises—or a field of crabgrass— neither one nor many, but always already a multiplicity. It thereby ever opens itself, in and through history, to the indeterminacies of negotiation within and across difference, precisely because it continues to "develop" in so many directions and ways, interacting with so many different contexts. Where a dominant language attempts to close upon itself by severing the lines of its own connective multiplicity (lines that are at once horizontal and vertical, spatial and temporal), theology may be rendered irrelevant to the salvation of the world, orthodoxy a dead letter if not a killing word.

For those of us who still hold some faith in theology, the faithfulness of theology itself must be rediscovered within the humility of its multiplicity, relinquishing the self-certainty of "knowing" and the desire to dominate. As ancient ascetics understood well, humility stands at the beginning of all striving for perfection: self-critique is the necessary precondition of the ambitious reach toward truth, as toward virtue (if we can still speak of "truth" or "virtue"). I would go so far as to say that the self-critical discourse of heresy should remain just that—a theological tool of self-reflection invoked in the service of humility in the face of all we cannot know, not a weapon to be wielded against others. We are all heretics, in other words, if that means that our understanding is always flawed. Here I wish to make common cause with Wiles's urging that doctrinal truth be ever pursued "in a consciously self-critical manner"[14]—a sentiment ambivalently echoed in Rowan Williams's insistence on the self-critical character of doctrine as "a 'text' already cognizant of its own ambiguities."[15] At the same time, with regard to Williams's

---

[12] Gilles Deleuze and Felix Guattari, *A Thousand Plateaus: Capitalism and Schizophrenia*, trans. Brian Massumi (Minneapolis, MN: University of Minnesota Press, 1987), 7–8.

[13] See Rowan Williams, "Does It Make Sense to Speak of Pre-Nicene Orthodoxy?" in *The Making of Orthodoxy: Essays in Honour of Henry Chadwick*, ed. Rowan Williams (Cambridge: Cambridge University Press, 1989), 1–23.

[14] Wiles, *The Remaking of Christian Doctrine*, 15.

[15] Rowan Williams, "Doctrinal Criticism: Some Questions," in *The Making and Remaking of Christian Doctrine: Essays in Honour of Maurice Wiles*, eds. Sarah Coakley and David A. Pailin

language, I worry about the possible fallacy introduced by the metaphor of doctrine as "a text." No more than it is *a* tree is doctrine *a* text, even if "text" is taken in a broad sense, as in the work of Michel Barnes and Lewis Ayres, who privilege not a particular creed, for example, but rather the "theological culture" of the fourth century as authoritatively orthodox.[16] For Barnes and Ayres, as for Williams, that fourth-century culture is a select one: it certainly does not include Arius, for example.[17] But what are the principles of selection? In a closing defense of his position, and with regard to the prior critiques of Nicene orthodoxy articulated by Maurice Wiles, Ayres hints that one could make a case that "pro-Nicene theology offers a more coherent reading of the plain sense of Scripture," yet, wisely perhaps, he does not attempt to do so: the sense of scripture has never been "plain" enough to avert theological difference or controversy. Ayres also gestures toward "the status of the Church and its teaching authority," acknowledging that church historians "are unlikely to demonstrate the continuity of doctrine's development" while suggesting that they should nonetheless try to do so, "for the good of the Church."[18] If the claim to identify a single, coherent "theological culture" in the fourth-century seems suspect from the historian's point of view, one might also ask on what basis one identifies "the Church" in our own moment or, for that matter, claims to know what is good for "it." True, as Wiles puts it, those who appropriate a theological voice must "affirm what seems to us to be true. We have to take our stand there; we can do no other."[19] Yet every theological stance taken requires that we take on the burden of demonstrating not only the internal logic and consistency of our affirmations but also their specific relevance and responsiveness to our particular contexts—what Wiles names the criteria of "coherence" and "economy."[20]

Doctrine is not, then, a text put on ice in the fourth century Mediterranean, or in any other time or place, but rather the ever-multiplying incarnational product of the ongoing textual practice of theology—a fantastically sprawling

---

(Oxford: Clarendon Press, 1993), 239–64; 250. Williams's position emerges out of a nuanced and respectful critique of the work of Maurice Wiles.

[16] Michel R. Barnes, "The Fourth Century as Trinitarian Canon," in *Christian Origins: Theology, Rhetoric, and Community*, eds. Lewis Ayres and Gareth Jones (London and New York: Routledge, 1998), 47–67; Lewis Ayres, *Nicaea and Its Legacy: An Approach to Fourth-Century Trinitarian Theology* (Oxford: Oxford University Press, 2004).

[17] See Rowan Williams, *Arius: Heresy and Tradition* (Grand Rapids, MI: Wm. B. Eerdmans Publishing Company, 2001; original, 1987), especially the *apologia* appearing in the revised edition as "Appendix I." Few contemporary historians of theology would argue that historical analysis can *in itself* demonstrate the "truth" of particular doctrinal assertions. Nonetheless, Williams, like Barnes and Ayres, seems to come very close to such a position, in so far as he claims to have shown via historical analysis both that Arius's ideas simply lost the competition for orthodoxy and thus disappeared, and that they were destined to do so, due to the identifiable inadequacies of his theology—both of these points, I believe, debatable on historical grounds.

[18] Ayres, *Nicaea and Its Legacy*, 428–29.

[19] Wiles, *The Remaking of Christian Doctrine*, 14.

[20] Ibid., 17–19.

and ever-mutating hypertext, perhaps. Its multiplicity is as irreducible as its connectivity, and both are the reflection of its historicity. By highlighting the historicity of doctrine, I do not mean to gesture toward its inevitable relativism—its unavoidable tendentiousness—with some ostensibly "postmodern" shrug of indifference. On the contrary, to locate doctrine as the effect of ongoing textual practice is to highlight its citational or iterative aspect and thus to look toward its continuous yet unpredictable persistence within time and also across place—to point toward the horizontality as well as the verticality of its complex and prolific root system. It is also to recall that textual repetition, like the rhizome, is the spatial and temporal matrix not only of connectivity but also of differentiation. No citation is exact or singular—the links between texts are multiple and multidirectional—and the impossibility of any exact or singular repetition is the condition for the liveliness as well as the faithfulness of doctrine qua apostolic tradition. Indeed, it is in the inexactitude of doctrinal repetition, the interval of creative difference, that the renewing work of the Spirit may be discovered.[21]

Apostolicity and Discipleship

The figure of the apostle so often invoked in antiquity to authorize orthodoxy is overlaid on the figure of the disciple—the *"beloved* disciple," as John's gospel has it, memorialized in the unforgettable pose of one nestled in his teacher's breast. Later Christians are invited to take on the role of the unnamed disciple, to lay their heads on the master's chest, to await his coming, to submit themselves to his love—to forget their own names, perhaps, like the martyrs who, when asked to identify themselves, will say only "I am a Christian." Witnesses in our own context might even need to forget they are Christians if they hope to become, once again, faithful followers of Christ rather than mere defenders of hardened identities. To love Jesus is to remember him, and to remember Jesus is also to forget oneself, to abandon oneself in and to the transformative power of love.

Sometimes it is also to compete for love. John's gospel anticipates later Christian texts in that it prickles with rivalry, most notably that between Peter and the beloved disciple, more subtly that between Peter and the beloved disciple, on the one hand, and Mary Magdalene, on the other. As the two men race each other to the master's tomb, Mary has already outpaced them. It is she who first encounters the risen Jesus, though she is cautioned not to attempt to hold onto him, in a famous and famously ambiguous scene. If the Gospel of John seems finally to privilege the love between men, even as it also generates competition between them, Mary's ambivalent role as first witness to the resurrection continues to complicate matters, interrupting the sublimely Platonic male homoeroticism also invoked by the gospel. Apostolic

---

[21] Cf. ibid., 10–14.

doctrine ever invites and requires the negotiation of multiplicity and frequently also a hermeneutic of suspicion directed toward any exclusive claims on the Lord—or on Lordship.

To remember is also to write and rewrite, to cite and recite—to record the traces of love's memory continuously. Perhaps only one who has fully submitted to love can author a gospel, can give witness to Jesus as master and teacher: thus, readers of John's gospel are quick to identify the beloved disciple with the writer of the text. Yet to write is also to forget, to allow the full presence of the divine word to be displaced by an inspired text and then subsequently by its inspired rereadings. A written memory is a relic; it is partial, fragmented, crucified, riddled with gaps to be filled by a reader who is open to the Spirit's penetration, who knows the arts of love required for interpretation. This Origen of Alexandria understood very well: for him, every reading of scripture is, potentially, an inspired reinscription of the Word of God that transforms both text and reader. "But there are also many other things which Jesus did; were every one of them to be written, I suppose that the world itself could not contain the books that would be written"— thus the last lines of John's gospel, announcing its own fragmentary status, remembering its own forgetfulness, ever awaiting the iterative excesses of readerly re-collection. (Gospel commentaries do seem to grow—and spread—like weeds.)

The concept of the apostle as preacher, guardian, or transmitter of an orthodox tradition originating with Jesus, on the one hand, and the concept of the apostle as a Christlike holy person, on the other, are never entirely separate. Discipleship, that eroticized relation of follower to teacher that is so central and persisting a feature of ancient culture, seems to hold these two concepts together from the start. If the understanding of the apostle as transmitter of a singular tradition leads to the production of an authoritative canon of scripture as well as of orthodox creeds and doctrinal traditions, the understanding of apostolicity as grounded in the imitation of Jesus is endlessly iterated in the memorializing production of martyrologies and hagiographies as well as in the ethical and ritual practices of Christians more generally. On the one side, we have truth, on the other, testimony. Yet can one separate truth from testimony, canon or creed from an iterative process of spiritual formation, in any ancient or contemporary Christian context known to us? To read the apostolic text of scripture is to encounter the Logos again and again, Origen insisted, and it is thereby also to be inscribed in a chain of apostolic succession, to become a successor of the apostles, a disciple of the disciples, by submitting to the endlessly transformative teaching of the text. It is, again loosely paraphrasing Origen, to remember precisely what was forgotten in the "fall," namely, how to love.

Where knowledge grasps once and for all, love touches—again and again. Where knowledge may be tempted to coerce and control, love can only hope to persuade and transform. History is appropriately partnered with theology not only because theology has a special relationship to the past but also precisely to the extent that history does not, and cannot, yield a single grasp-able or grasping truth. The past will always elude us: we can only capture fragmentary shards of its dazzling otherness in our thickest descriptions, tug at isolated strands of its dense, subterranean networks of causality in our most sophisticated analyses. Similarly, theology (for those who still elect to trust in it) repeatedly touches upon, yet can never grasp, truths enfolded by—and unfolding within—the veils of time and place.

Orthodoxy and Polydoxy

Recently, "polydoxy" has been proposed as an alternative, or perhaps an antidote, to orthodoxy, embracing—rather than repressing—the multiplicity, open-endedness, and relationality of both the practice and the object of theology. Clearly, such a framing resonates strongly with the brief reflections on history and theology that I have offered here. However, where the dis-course of orthodoxy tends to suppress its own inevitable, ongoing novelty, polydoxy—as proclaimed by the editors and contributors to the volume of the same name—may risk overstating its novelty, as if this were anything but inevitable. In so doing, and against their own best intentions, polydoxy's advocates may find themselves, not unlike Bauer, having not so much deconstructed the discourse of orthodoxy as inverted it, thereby making a heresy of orthodoxy and instating polydoxy as . . . well, yet another ortho-doxy announcing the triumph over false belief—or rather, in this case, the triumph over the falseness of belief as such. To be sure, the editors of the *Polydoxy* volume, as well as its contributors, are well aware of this possibility and set out to distance themselves from it from the start. Repeatedly, and with welcome nuance, they acknowledge that, "like other global religions, 'Chris-tianity' was never really One to begin with. Internally multiple and complex, it has always required an agile and spirited approach to theological reflec-tion." But is there no danger in the very gesture of coining a "nickname" (as they dub it) that might seem to serve as the rallying cry or the banner of a new theological "movement"?[22]

We live in an era in which the forces of change and novelty, diversity and difference, are undeniable. This experience and the sensibility to which this gives rise is scarcely unprecedented, as any student of the late Roman empire, for example, is well aware; nor is it easily separable from the very forces of imperialism and globalization that seem so often intent on suppressing and flattening diversity and difference, then as now. Still, the particularity, and the particular intensity, of our moment must be honored, and the *Polydoxy* volume does this very beautifully indeed, not least by bringing Christian

---

[22] Catherine Keller and Laurel Schneider, "Introduction," *Polydoxy: Theology of Multiplicity and Relation* (New York: Routledge, 2011), 1–2.

theology intimately and fluidly into dialogue with a wide range of contemporary philosophical and theoretical discourses drawn from globally dispersed contexts. Newman himself affirmed that the development of theological doctrine "depends in various ways on the circumstances around it":[23] "whatever be the risk of corruption from intercourse with the world around it, such a risk must be undergone," as he puts it, adding that "to live is to change and to be perfect is to have changed often."[24] Would he have approved of the idea of "polydoxy" as such? Hardly. Yet the logic of his thought suggests that doctrine might develop an explicit and articulated, or "conscious," awareness its own malleability and multiplicity precisely as a result of such "circumstances around it," and that in so doing it *might* not be breaking with the past—introducing "corruption"—so much as bringing past insights to greater maturity and completeness of expression. My aim is not to make such a case but simply to consider the possibility that polydoxy, when invoked as a rallying cry, may not have strayed very far from (at least some versions of) orthodoxy, not only insofar as it has not altogether escaped orthodoxy's binarism, but also insofar as it has not altogether rejected the progressivist historiographic principles by which Newman attempted to make peace between history and theology. How much of a problem is this? This remains to be seen.

Conceptually and descriptively, polydoxy might be of significant use to historians as well as theologians. Yet its primary location within theological discourse draws it toward normative pronouncement in some ways that might trouble many historians and should perhaps also trouble even friendly-minded theologians just a little bit. Can there be a polydoxy that does not need to announce its triumph over the heresy of orthodoxy? Can there be a polydoxy that does not proclaim to supersede what has come before? Can there be a polydoxy moved above all by humility and love? I hope so, and for the most part this volume greatly strengthens my hope. Both because of and despite their occasional penchant for rhetorical exuberance, the contributors to *Polydoxy* arguably begin to show us not only what "a theology of multiplicity and relation" might look like in the ever-emerging future, but also how it has also always been a part of history—as measured both horizontally and vertically, across differences of both time and space.

---

[23] Newman, *Essay*, 99.
[24] Ibid., 100.

Modern Theology 30:3 July 2014
ISSN 0266-7177 (Print)
ISSN 1468-0025 (Online)

DOI: 10.1111/moth.12119

TRADITION ON FIRE: POLYDOXY, ORTHODOXY, AND THEOLOGICAL EPISTEMOLOGY

SHANNON CRAIGO-SNELL

Coming to Terms

One of the gifts of the volume *Polydoxy: Theology of Multiplicity and Relation*, is the introduction of a new meaning of the term "polydoxy" into contemporary theology. This term is not distinctly defined, but rather performed in thirteen essays. The essays are introduced as "performances of polydoxy."[1] The resulting volume is neither a genealogy nor a dictionary entry, but rather a collection of examples of a "mode" of constructive theology (Keller and Schneider, "Introduction," 13). The meaning of polydoxy, as performed in these various essays, coheres in appreciation for multiplicity, unknowing (or open-endedness), and relationality (Keller and Schneider, "Introduction," 4). This coherence cannot be separated from other ways the essays stick together, namely in the palpable influence of postmodernism, postcolonial theory, and process theology. Throughout the text, there are playful treatments of the terms that give the word "polydoxy" both substance and friction. Poly, meaning many, is brought together with pli, as in multiplicity, evoking a plurality that is not composed of individual ones (Keller and Schneider, "Introduction," 2; see also Keller, "Be a multiplicity: ancestral anticipations," 87). Doxa, meaning thought, appearance, opinion, or glory, is valued for its excessive and slippery possible denotations (See Rivera, "Glory: the first

Shannon Craigo-Snell
Louisville Presbyterian Theological Seminary, 1044 Alta Vista Road, Louisville, KY 40205, USA
Email: scraigo-snell@lpts.edu

[1] Catherine Keller and Laurel C. Schneider, "Introduction," in Catherine Keller and Laurel C. Schneider (eds), *Polydoxy: Theology of Multiplicity and Relation* (New York: Routledge, 2010), 4. Subsequent references to *Polydoxy* will be cited internally according to author, title and page number.

passion of theology?" 167–85). And of course, "orthodoxy" hangs in the air. The term polydoxy itself, and the multiple performances of polydoxy in this volume, come to be in intentional relation to orthodoxy. Thus a second gift of this text is the opportunity to consider carefully what "orthodoxy" means. The authors resist a strict binary opposition between polydoxy and orthodoxy, and they acknowledge that orthodoxy is also multiple. However, I argue that the volume—whether inadvertently or inescapably—functionally reduces orthodoxy to a single epistemological viewpoint, which I will describe as the Logic of the One. This has two drawbacks. First, it is inadequate to the multiplicity of Christian orthodoxies. Second, polydoxy itself is limited. Polydoxy performed in connection to a single orthodoxy will be less multiple, open-ended, and relational than polydoxy performed in connection to multiple orthodoxies.

What is Orthodoxy?

The authors of *Polydoxy: Theology of Multiplicity and Relation* are careful not to portray Christianity as singular or monolithic (Keller and Schneider, "Introduction," 2,). Several essays point out the polydoxy of traditional Christianity, the multiplicity and relation inherent in Biblical narratives and Christian interpretations (Keller and Schneider, "Introduction," 2, 9, 12; see also Schneider, "Crib notes from Bethlehem," 33). The introduction to the volume states, "The Christian tradition is always already polydox" (Keller and Schneider, "Introduction," 2). Furthermore, the editors note that "much theology that has been understood as orthodox nourishes and advances its own polydox legacy" (Keller and Schneider, "Introduction," 2). Such statements reflect the constructive use of Christian traditions being made by the authors themselves. Polydoxy, in these essays, is performed in creative continuity with Christianity's own resistance to univocity.

At the same time, polydoxy is performed in critique—sometimes explicit, sometimes implicit—of orthodoxy. What is meant by orthodoxy here? The diversity of these numerous texts makes it difficult to say, exactly, even as the term "orthodoxy" appears to have a persistent, coherent valence throughout the volume. In common parlance, orthodoxy often refers to the boundaries of belief or action placed by ecclesial authority. This kind of ecclesial orthodoxy is mentioned a few times in the book. For example, Marion Grau's excellent essay, "Signs taken for polydoxy in a Zulu Kraal," discusses the heresy trial of Bishop John William Colenso, who, among other things, argued that polygamy among the Zulu was not necessarily sinful (Grau, "Signs taken for polydoxy in Zulu Kraal," 221, 228). Yet issues of ecclesiastical orthodoxy are mentioned too rarely to be the primary concerns of this text. Actual lives are bruised and scraped by bumping into church dictates regarding the ordination of women, the status of same-sex love, the possibilities of procreation and contraception, and many other issues. Such concrete suffering would surely be more central to this volume if polydoxy were understood primarily in relationship to this kind of ecclesial orthodoxy. Instead of addressing concrete instanciations of ecclesial orthodoxy, the introduction critiques the "habit of producing heretics as outer boundary markers for orthodox identity" (Keller and Schneider, "Introduction," 2).

Dictionary definitions of orthodoxy tend to emphasize adherence to dogma and creeds. Yet, in a similar pattern, the authors spend little time engaging particular dogmas or addressing the complex tensions of creedal formulations. The volume is not framed to take issue with any particular dogma, put rather with any and all "dogmatic certainty" (Keller and Schneider, "Introduction," 7). Much of the volume is concerned not with particular ecclesial or dogmatic orthodoxies, but rather with dogmatic certainty that is used to produce heretics. This certainty is sustained by an epistemology that sees Truth as singular and universal, and therefore has no room for different views. I conclude that polydoxy is positioned in relation to the very idea of orthodoxy—the abstract concept of doxa (thought, appearance, glory) being single—especially when this singularity is used to create outer boundaries and repress other views.

This notion of orthodoxy is given further nuance and content when it is referred to as the "orthodoxy of the One" (Keller and Schneider, "Introduction," 2). I take this to be a reference to the work of feminist theorist Luce Irigaray, among others. It evokes a particular Western mindset in which truth is understood as singular, universal, and anchored by a monotheistic god. Three characteristics of this "logic of the One" (Grau, "Signs taken for polydoxy in Zulu Kraal," 220) are particularly salient to this discussion. First, in this framework identity is constructed and secured through binary opposition which is then repressed or forgotten. For example, the meaning of "light" is understood in opposition to the meaning of "dark," the meaning of "in" is understood in opposition to the meaning of "out," "women" are understood as the opposite of "men," and so on. While opposition is needed for differentiation between members of each pair, real difference is ultimately repressed. "Dark" is understood as not really the opposite, but rather the absence of "light." "Out" is to not be "in" and "women" are defective or deficient "men." Difference—needed at first to secure identity—is diminished into gradations that are amenable to hierarchy. There are no apples and oranges that cannot be compared. All fruit—all being!—can be ranked as greater or lesser links in a single great chain. Thus Irigaray reads Western culture from Plato onward, and particularly in its modern forms, as permeated by a logic of Sameness in which everything can be compared and ordered.[2] Truth, Being, the Good, God—some singular ultimate marked by a

---

[2] This brief and inadequate summary of some of Irigaray's work is derived from Luce Irigaray, "Plato's Hystera" in Gillian C. Gill (trans) *Speculum of the Other Woman* (Ithaca, NY: Cornell University Press, 1985), 243–364.

capital letter—is both fount and anchor of all lesser truths, beings, and goodness.

Second, Irigaray emphasizes that this kind of logic requires a dualistic view of mind and body. Bodies are concrete, specific, and located. They clearly are not universal, nor universally similar. There are lots of different bodies around, and embodied persons each see, sense, and feel things differently. Whole-personed knowing—that acknowledges the intertwining of body, mind, emotion, and will—challenges the always-and-everywhere abstract, universal Truth that is central to the logic of the One. So the human person is divided. Mind and body are first seen as opposites, in order to clearly identify each. Then this difference is repressed, such that the body becomes a functionary of the mind. What is essential to the human person is the rational mind, which is capable of knowing the singular truth. The many ways in which human bodies know must be forgotten or disabled in order for a singular system of value to hold sway.

Third, the logic of the One is learned. It is not a natural system, hardwired into the universe, but rather a culturally produced mindset into which we are trained. Only a thorough, systematic indoctrination into this way of seeing the world makes the whole set-up seem natural, given, and obvious. Seeing clearly in this light is an acquired skill, a disciplined forgetting of other ways of knowing. In the book *Speculum of the Other Woman*, Irigaray retells the story of Plato's cave as one of a successive educational blinding. The shackled prisoners at first see by the light of "a *fire* burning at a distance, behind and above them."[3] One prisoner is selected and taken up a path, looking at brighter and brighter lights in the movement towards the surface, eventually gazing upon the Sun itself. Instead of reading this as a path to greater sight and clarity, Irigaray interprets this as a painful process in which the prisoner is taught to see and know in only one particular way. The prisoner is methodically blinded to other ways of knowing, particularly ways that involve bodies, the earth, and difference. In Irigaray's words, "the sight of the sun . . . runs a strong risk of putting out bodily eyes from their sockets."[4] Eventually, the Sun appears to the well-trained student as the only possible light, the single, self-evident Truth. Being educated into this photological epistemology is a process of learning to see by a single light. It is this orthodoxy that supplies the background of *Polydoxy*.

Traditional Fires

While the influence of the Logic of the One spans centuries, it gets a serious reboot in the early modern West. One of the easiest places to spy this logic at work is in the writings of René Descartes as he grapples with ways of

---

[3] Ibid., 245.
[4] Ibid., 305.

knowing, old and new. Descartes sat by a fire in Germany in 1619. Dissatisfied with received wisdom in matters of science and philosophy, he began a personal discipline of doubt, razing the edifice of his own knowledge in order to build anew on sure foundations. Sitting alone in a stove-heated room, Descartes devised four rules to help him set aside everything he once believed and embark on an ordered process of investigation. He would start with the simplest objects, dividing topics as need be, and accept only clear and distinct ideas that could not be doubted, eventually creating a comprehensive view of each issue considered. He began with lines and proportions, settling the problems of geometry and algebra to his own satisfaction within a few months. Before the winter was fully over, Descartes left the fireside to travel and continue his task "in discussions with other people."[5] Nine years later his reputation exceeded his success, prompting Descartes to return to solitude to continue his intellectual quest. Alone again, Descartes settled in to determined doubtfulness, letting go of ideas and beliefs that came from his senses, from logical arguments, and from his own thoughts. He found what he could not doubt was his own thinking, thus, "I think, therefore I am."[6]

Descartes moves quickly and confidently from this discovery to positive certainty regarding the rational soul and the existence of God. Unable to doubt that he is thinking or to stop thinking, he declares himself to be "a substance, the whole essence or nature of which was to think."[7] Furthermore, because he can imagine himself without a body, he states that the rational soul and the body are "completely distinct" and that "even if the body did not exist the soul would still be everything that it is."[8] Descartes continues to reflect on his doubting. He sees clearly that to know is more perfect than to doubt. He then wonders, where did he get the idea of something more perfect than himself? He reasons that he could not have learned of a being more perfect than himself from nothing, nor from himself. He concludes, "this idea was put in me by a nature that was really more perfect than I was, one that even had in itself all the perfections of which I could have some idea, that is—to express myself in a single word—by God."[9] The God thus deduced is singular, perfect, and simple, since composition or dependence of any kind is a defect for Descartes. God allows Descartes to trust his own thinking, anchoring and stabilizing both reason and the world.[10]

In a few short pages within the *Discourse on Method*, Descartes both states and models epistemological assumptions that were to become mainstream in

---

[5] René Descartes, "Discourse on the Method for Guiding One's Reason and Searching for Truth in the Sciences" in Desmond D. Clarke (trans), *Discourse on Method and Related Writings* (London: Penguin Books, 1999), 22.

[6] Ibid., 25.

[7] Ibid.

[8] Ibid.

[9] Ibid., 26.

[10] Ibid, 28–29. See also 31.

much of the modern West. He affirms that reason "is naturally equal in all human beings."[11] Each person has reason, a God-given "light for distinguishing what is true from what is false."[12] However, this laudably egalitarian view is part and parcel of a larger worldview in which there is little room for difference to be valued positively. For Descartes, there is only one truth on any given subject.[13] Diversity of opinion implies error.[14] Descartes takes geometry as his model for truth—the angles of a triangle will always add up to 180°, regardless of who does the calculations. The certainty Descartes experiences in geometry is what he hopes for in all of his life. The way to attain that certainty, as modeled by Descartes, is to let go of received wisdom and the authority of books. Instead, travel and think for yourself. Then, sit alone. Distance yourself from your community. Do not be guided by your ethical commitments—a provisional ethics, taken from the moderates around you, will serve until you have worked out your own with certainty.[15] Abstract yourself from your own embodiment. Thus goes Descartes' attempt at thinking well. He is convinced that if we all thought really well (along the lines that he himself attempts), we would arrive at the same conclusions and embrace the same self-evident Truth.

At this point, the lurking downside to Descartes' egalitarianism comes into play. If we are all fundamentally the same (reasonable creatures created by the same God and striving for the same singular Truth), then our differences are simply matters of degree. We can be compared and valued on a single scale according to how well we fulfill our common nature, how clearly we grasp the universal Truth. Unfortunately, the hierarchical implications of some of Descartes' assumptions are familiar. People associated more with bodies than with minds—including women, African-Americans, and manual laborers—are seen as slightly less human. Within a Cartesian frame, kinds of knowledge that involve embodiment—including action, ritual, and dance—are difficult to recognize as knowledge at all. Read in this particular way, Descartes' *Discourse on Method* can serve as a concrete illustration of the Logic of the One diagnosed by Irigaray. Sitting by a fire, Descartes came to see Irigaray's blinding, self-evident sun.

Yet the stove that heated Descartes' room throughout the German winter was not the only fire blazing in early modern Europe. A quite different character, George Fox, sat fireside in England in 1648. Fox was one of the founders of the Religious Society of Friends, commonly called Quakers. Although Fox was not as well-educated as Descartes, both men breathed the air of early modernism. Like Descartes, Fox found the traditional authorities

---

[11] Ibid., 5.
[12] Ibid., 22.
[13] Ibid., 10.
[14] Ibid., 10, 13.
[15] Ibid., 19.

of his day wanting and turned from studying to travel and personal exploration. He also believed that God has given each person an inner Light by
which to know the truth, although he did not identify this Light with reason.
Fox even participated in the language of the emerging scientific method,
describing knowledge gleaned from his religious experience as knowledge
gained "experimentally."[16] While the knowledge thus gained did not offer the
universal certainty of mathematics as Descartes desired, Fox also found that
which he could rely upon with confidence. He describes his own fireside
epiphany, an epistemological conversion that shapes his view of how human
beings know:

> One morning, as I was sitting by the fire, a great cloud came over me, and
> a temptation beset me; and I sat still. It was said, "All things come by
> nature"; and the elements and stars came over me, so that I was in a
> manner quite clouded with it. But as I sat still and said nothing, the
> people of the house perceived nothing. And as I sat still under it and let
> it alone, a living hope and a true voice arose in me, which said, "There is
> a living God who made all things." Immediately the cloud and tempta-
> tion vanished away, and life rose over it all; my heart was glad, and I
> praised the living God.[17]

Fox's fireside moment is quite different from Descartes.' Quaker theologian R. Melvin Keiser contrasts the two accounts, noting that this scene does
not unfold at Fox's instigation.[18] He is responding to the world around him.
Descartes engages in a methodical, rational act of doubt, while Fox experiences temptation and waits—in hope and trust—for something deeper than
rationality to rise.[19] The Inner Light that guides Fox is not known in abstraction from community and commitment, but within those. The Quaker spirituality of Fox, Keiser asserts, begins with a "non-dualistic starting point of
divine depth emerging to human surface."[20] Quakerism does not begin with
dualism between God and humanity, between body and spirit, between men
and women, between fallen world and new creation, or between Christianity
and all other religious traditions.[21] Likewise, there is in Fox's Journal and in
Quakerism a non-dualistic approach to the relationships between individual
and community and between public and private.

There are many ways in which the Religious Society of Friends in the
seventeenth century distilled the ideals of early modernity into a religious

---

[16] George Fox, *The Journal of George Fox*, Rufus M. Jones (ed), (Richmond, IN: Friends United Press, 1976), 82.
[17] Ibid., 94.
[18] R. Melvin Keiser, "Theological Groping: Toward Postcritical Spirituality in Modern Culture and Quaker Roots," unpublished paper, 7.
[19] Ibid., 7.
[20] Ibid., 8.
[21] Ibid., 8, 10, 11.

community. They stood out from their contemporaries by embracing such ideals even more fully than most. While many early modern authors wrote about an inner light, given by God to help human persons discern knowledge, Quakers took this affirmation so seriously that it drastically shaped their worship and governance. All persons were given inner Light, therefore all were seen as equal—not just theoretically so, but practically, such that women could speak in worship and men no longer tipped their hats to social superiors. Traditional religious authority structures were critiqued and replaced by more egalitarian leadership, without ordained clergy. Books were no longer seen as the ideal source of knowledge; even Biblical authority was diminished in deference to lived experience and the tutelage of the Light within. Finally, Quakers shared the early modern sensibility that true worship was not a matter of ritual, but rather of spiritual worship and ethical life. This, too, Quakers took farther than most, eschewing cathedrals for bare meeting-houses and liturgy for silent worship. In all of these ways, Quakers were quintessentially modern.

Yet the Logic of the One, with binary oppositions that get repressed into sameness, is not dominant in Fox's fire, not a driving force in this originary moment of Quakerism. There is not a defining dualism between Creator and creation. The God Fox acknowledges does not serve as a perfect stabilizer for human knowledge. Instead, there is "a living God" interconnected with "all things." Something of this God is known when "a living hope and a true voice" arise within Fox, both immanent and transcendent, and "life" rises over all.[22] The epistemology of Fox and the egalitarianism of seventeenth-century Quakerism illuminate a different logic at play within early modern European Christianity, a logic in which "one" and "many" are living and dynamic terms rather than binary opposites.

Fox's fireside temptation is recorded within his *Journal*, which was edited, published, and distributed to Quaker communities after Fox's death, at his instruction and expense. The *Journal* was a scandal to many at the time of its publication, since Fox records several occasions of miraculously curing the sick, while omitting any acknowledgement of his own sin. The *Journal* did not become a basic text of academic philosophy. Instead, its pages have had enormous spiritual and literary influence upon writers such as Wordsworth, Coleridge, Longfellow, Emerson, George Bernard Shaw and William James.[23] Another reader of Fox's Journal was Elias Hicks, a Quaker preacher, whom Walt Whitman heard preach many times. Long before "I contain multitudes," Whitman wrote, "Always Elias Hicks gives the service of pointing to the fountain of all naked theology, all religion, all worship, all the truth to which

---

[22] Fox, *Journal*, 94.
[23] Henry J. Cadbury, "The Influence of Journal of George Fox," in George Fox, *The Journal of George Fox*, Rufus M. Jones (ed), (Richmond, IN: Friends United Press, 1976), 10, 13, 14, 16.

you are possibly eligible—namely *yourself* and your inherent relations."[24] Whitman found wisdom in Fox's unusual, non-dualistic account of relations between God and humanity. Fully aware of the enormous contrast between the two, Whitman compared Fox to Shakespeare. He wrote, "What is poor plain George Fox compared to William Shakspere [sic]—to fancy's lord, imagination's heir? Yet George Fox stands for something too—a thought—the thought that wakes in silent hours—perhaps the deepest, most eternal thought latent in the human soul. This is the thought of God, merged in the thoughts of moral right and the immortality of identity."[25]

One more fire can be brought into relation with the fires of Descartes and Fox. Few specifics are known about the two-hour conflagration that took place Monday, November 23, 1654.The only record was found on a piece of parchment sewn into the lining of Blaise Pascal's coat, discovered after his death in Paris in 1662.

Fire
"God of Abraham, God of Isaac, God of Jacob," not of philosophers and scholars
Certainty, certainty, heartfelt, joy, peace.
God of Jesus Christ.
God of Jesus Christ.
My God and your God.
"Thy God shall be my God."
The world forgotten, and everything except God.
He can only be found by the ways taught in the Gospels.
Greatness of the human soul.
"O righteous Father, the world had not known thee, but I have known thee."
Joy, joy, joy, tears of joy.
I have cut myself off from him.
They have forsaken me, the fountain of living waters.
"My God wilt thou forsake me?"
Let me not be cut off from him for ever!
"And this is life eternal, that they might know thee, the only true God, and Jesus Christ whom thou hast sent."
Jesus Christ.
Jesus Christ.
I have cut myself off from him, shunned him, denied him, crucified him.
Let me never be cut off from him!
He can only be kept by the ways taught in the Gospel.

---

[24] Walt Whitman, "As Myself a Little Boy," http://www2.gol.com/users/quakers/walt _whitman.htm, accessed September 8, 2013.
[25] Walt Whitman, "V. November Boughs, George Fox (and Shakspere)" http://www.bartleby .com/229/5022.html, accessed September 8, 2013.

Sweet and total renunciation.
Total submission to Jesus Christ and my director.
Everlasting joy in return for one day's effort on earth.
I will not forget thy word. Amen.[26]

Pascal describes a momentous event, about which the first thing he could say was "FIRE." From and in this event, he learned about the God of Abraham, Isaac, and Jacob. Not the God of logical deduction and reasoned proofs, not a living God whose voice rises within him, but the God described in the sacred texts of Jews and Christians, the God that Pascal believed to be incarnate in Jesus of Nazareth. This text, filled with emotion and scriptural references, offers a different view of knowing and knowledge than that of Descartes or Fox. Pascal knows, with both certainty and joy, in submission, renunciation, confession, and relationship. He knows the "righteous Father," the "God of Jesus Christ."[27]

This fire is also an epistemological conversion, quite different from those of Descartes and Fox. Pascal was a brilliant mathematician who made significant contributions in the development of probability theory and calculus. Like Descartes, he honored the logic of geometry and valued certainty. However, Pascal did not make mathematical and geometrical logic the pattern for all knowledge.[28] Not just the mind, but also the heart and the body have roles to play in knowledge, particularly in knowledge of God.[29] Like Fox, Pascal has a strong sense of revelation. God makes Godself known to humanity. However, for Pascal this is approached within a church structure and tradition that understands who God is primarily through historical revelation attested in Scripture.

Furthermore, unlike Descartes and Fox, Pascal expresses a strong sense of sin. His writings are not filled with optimism about human knowledge of God. Pascal understands God to be incomprehensible by human intellect, and he understands human intellect to be clouded by sin.[30] He writes, "True religion teaches us our duties, our weaknesses, pride and concupiscence, and the remedies, humility and mortification."[31] Both the glory of God and the sinfulness of humanity mean that we cannot be as sanguine about knowledge of God as we can about mathematical equations or geometric formulations.

These three fireside epiphanies took place within 45 years and 600 miles of each other. And they are connected by more than time and geography. Pascal

---

[26] Blaise Pascal, *Pensées*, A. J. Krailsheimer (trans) (London: Penguin Books, 1966), 285–86.
[27] Ibid., 185.
[28] Ibid., 28–29. For a discussion of this, see Frederick Copleston, S.J., *A History of Philosophy Volume VI: Modern Philosophy from Descartes to Leibniz* (New York: Doubleday, 1960), 157–63.
[29] Pascal, *Pensées*, 28, 247–48.
[30] See ibid., 117.
[31] Ibid., 69.

argued against Descartes, who responded in kind; the two met on a couple of occasions.[32] Anne Conway, whose salon is described in Catherine Keller's essay (81–101), knew both Descartes and Fox; Queen Christina of Sweden knew both Descartes and Pascal. Voltaire wrote about all three men, and each has had profound influence on modernity and modern Christianity. Placing them side by side can be useful in understanding both the polydoxy of traditional Christianity and the multiplicity of orthodoxy itself.

Which Orthodoxy?

First and foremost, these three episodes illustrate the variety within Christian traditions, specifically in regards to theological epistemology. While similar in many ways, Descartes, Fox, and Pascal each offer remarkably different views of what knowledge of God looks like and how it is attained. In a traditional reading of Descartes, God can be deduced from human cognition and serves to stabilize the same. For Fox, God is known through ongoing personal revelation that cannot be separated from community and ethical commitments. For Pascal, in so much as God is known, it is in relationship with Jesus Christ, involving body, mind, and heart in church practices. Imagine how many faithful fires we could find if we looked a bit farther in both time and space, throughout the centuries and continents in which Christian communities have flourished. It is also worth noting that all of these authors have been enfolded, to some extent, into the mainstream of Western Christianity by the beginning of the twenty-first century. Stated somewhat differently, these writers have been incorporated, to greater or lesser degrees, into the Western canon. Second, each of these authors encountered orthodoxy in his life, if we understand orthodoxy to be the creation of "outer boundary" markers for Christian identity. Each of these men was on the edge of heresy, as defined by his particular context. And yet, the orthodoxies they faced were quite distinct. Descartes, Fox, and Pascal faced three different forms of Christian normative authority, confrontations that resulted in concrete repercussions in their lives.

Descartes, an observant Catholic, treads carefully around issues of epistemological certainty in the *Discourse on Method*. Engaging scientific method rather than relying on Aristotelian demonstrations, Descartes, like Galileo, was supporting a method of research sanctioned by neither the church nor the academy.[33] He knew his writing might cause conflicts. When he composed a heliocentric manuscript titled *The World; or, Treatise on Light*, Descartes chose to write about an imaginary world, very similar to ours, rather than engage directly in current cosmological debates. He later explained, "in order to camouflage all these things to some extent and to be

---

[32] A. J. Krailsheimer, "Introduction," in Blaise Pascal, *Pensées*, xiii.
[33] Descartes, *Discourse*, xxi.

able to say more freely what I thought about them without having either to accept or refute the views that are in vogue among the learned, I decided to leave this whole real world to their disputes and to speak only about what would happen in a new world if God were to create somewhere, in imaginary space. . . ."[34] After Galileo's condemnation by the Roman Inquisition, Descartes decided even writing about a hypothetical world was not enough discursive cover and he cancelled his plans to publish the text.[35] Galileo was suspected of heresy and forced to recant. The contention between the church and Galileo, and thus the worry for Descartes, was about both heliocentrism and the authority of scientific method. The issues were the centrality of the Sun and epistemology. In order to contend with a concrete and menacing form of ecclesial orthodoxy, Descartes had to alter his writing and publishing.

Pascal was a Roman Catholic involved directly with a different form of orthodoxy. Through family circumstances, Pascal was introduced to the theology of Cornelius Jansenius and became involved with the community centered at Port-Royal, an abbey in Paris. Pascal's sister Jacqueline joined the convent at Port-Royal in 1652. Although he was initially hesitant about his sister's decision, Pascal's own ties to the Jansenist community strengthened considerably after his "fire" event in 1654.[36] Port-Royal was the center of a movement within the Roman Catholic Church that (following Jansenius' reading of Augustine) emphasized human sinfulness and the necessity of grace, while de-emphasizing human free will in the process of salvation. Pascal became embroiled in a dispute between Jesuits and Jansenists.[37] He defended the Jansenists against Pope Innocent X's condemnation of Five Propositions that were allegedly contained within Jansenius' writings. It was a long, drawn-out, and complex affair, raising issues of doctrine, textual interpretation, and the limits of theological exploration within Roman Catholic tradition. The orthodoxy Pascal encountered was both dogmatic and ecclesial, an internal argument among Roman Catholics about finer points of theology and the authority of the magisterium.

This orthodoxy mattered a great deal to Pascal in his own life. He was deeply distressed by the Jansenists' defeat in this conflict. At the same time, he was unwilling to break with the Catholic Church. Weakened by the illness from which he would soon die, Pascal realized "that continued membership of the Catholic Church was incompatible with disobedience to the most formal orders of the Pope and hierarchy [therefore] Pascal submitted unconditionally and recognized himself incompetent to pronounce unilaterally on matters of faith."[38] This capitulation on a theological argument ought not be

---

[34] Ibid., 31.
[35] Ibid., xvi.
[36] Copleston, *History of Philosophy*, 153; Krailsheimer, "Introduction," xiii.
[37] His arguments appear in the *Provincial Letters*; see Copleston, *History of Philosophy*, 156.
[38] Krailsheimer, "Introduction," xvii.

read as superficial agreement in order to remain within the community. Pascal's fireside epiphany values the authority of the church and the virtue of submission in matters of religious knowledge. His theological epistemology emerged within, and remained consistent with, ecclesial structures that enforced boundaries.

Fox's conflicts with orthodoxy were markedly different from those of Descartes and Pascal, in part because he was not a Roman Catholic. Seventeenth-century England was a place of intense political conflict and increasing religious diversity. In addition to Roman Catholic and Church of England congregations, Presbyterians and Independents, there were also Baptists and Anabaptists, Muggletonians, Ranters, Seekers, and more. In a text called *Heresiographie*, published in 1645, Ephraim Pagit wrote of Familists, Sabbatarians, Anti-Sabbatarians, Traskites, Millenaries, and Etheringtonians.[39] The challenged and unsteady orthodoxy of the Church of England tried to secure itself through force. It was impossible, within such a time of turmoil, to neatly separate religious, social, and political actions. Yet it is clear that Fox's behavior was judged to be a threat on many levels. On religious grounds, Fox was beaten and stoned by crowds for his preaching, arrested for interrupting a sermon, and jailed for blasphemy.[40] On social grounds, he suffered repeated physical punishments and imprisonments for actions that challenged the social hierarchy of England. And on political grounds, he was sent to the dungeon for refusing to become a soldier and arrested on suspicion of plotting armed revolt against Oliver Cromwell.[41] The kind of orthodoxy Fox encountered was a wild, peculiar mix of theology, culture, and politics.

His own theology was deeply shaped by the oppressive orthodoxy he encountered. The Religious Society of Friends is most well-known for its profound Peace Testimony, a witness against war. This testimony is rooted in Fox's commitment to live in the Light of God, "in the virtue of that life and power that took away the occasion of all wars."[42] It is also rooted, to some degree, in the desire of early Friends to avoid conscription and suspicion in the religiously-freighted violence of Fox's day. The heart of the Quaker Peace Testimony is this: "All bloody principles and practices, we, as to our own particulars, do utterly deny, with all outward wars and strife and fightings with outward weapons, for any end or under any pretence whatsoever. And this is our testimony to the whole world."[43] These words appeared in a declaration given to King Charles II, in which Friends identified themselves

---

[39] *Heresiography, or a description and history of the hereticks and sectaries sprang up in these latter times*, by Ephraim Pagit, sixth edition (London: Ptd. for William Lee, 1661), 13.

[40] Ibid., 107, 52–3.

[41] Ibid., 54, 178–79.

[42] George Fox, *Journal of George Fox*, John L. Nickalls (ed) (London: Religious Society of Friends, 1975), 65.

[43] Fox, *Journal*, 399.

as "harmless and innocent people of God."[44] This declaration was both a prophetic theological claim and a straightforward attempt to clear Quakers from allegations that they were plotting against the King, to get Friends released from prison, and to avoid forced military service.

Descartes, Pascal, and Fox know God by the lights of their own, distinct fires and in relation to their encounters with distinct orthodoxies. The *Polydoxy* authors acknowledge, celebrate, and learn from the multiplicity within Christianity. Orthodoxy—even repressive, normative, Christian boundary-making—is also multiple. The orthodoxy in relation to which polydoxy is performed appears singular. Polydoxy is not cast in relation to ecclesial orthodoxy or dogmatic orthodoxy, but rather in relation to theoretical orthodoxy, understood as the Logic of the One. Can we appreciate the differences in these three fires if we do not acknowledge the variety of oppressive orthodoxies that would have quenched them?

Setting a Fire in School

Reading *Polydoxy*, it seems the vast variety of Christian conflagrations have all been threatened by the drenching brightness of the Sun. The possible exception is Descartes' stove. Descartes' epistemology can be read as partaking of the Logic of the Same. It is an orthodoxy of Truth, singular and universal, attained by an individual sitting alone, abstracted from embodiment, ethical commitment, and community. In both Descartes' account and Irigaray's analysis, this orthodoxy is anchored by a single deity who secures singular knowing.[45] Oddly enough, the view Descartes feared would be seen as heresy in his context exemplifies what is meant by "orthodoxy" in *Polydoxy: Theology of Multiplicity and Relation*.

There are good reasons to focus on the Logic of the Same as orthodoxy. First, it is pervasive. One could make the argument that all instances of ecclesial and dogmatic orthodoxy are ultimately rooted in the theoretical orthodoxy of the One—that the base problem is about singularity of Truth and if this were resolved, all orthodoxies would wither away. Second, it is particularly damaging to Christian theology. Descartes' legacy illustrates this point. His epistemological values—objective, always-and-everywhere Truth known through reason abstracted from embodiment and community—are woefully unsuited to the complex, multiple, and incarnate reality of Christian traditions. An enormous amount of Christianity—including rituals and sacraments, devotion and discipline, prayers and potlucks—are hard to value within a Cartesian frame. These aspects of Christian life are embodied, communal, and committed. As such they cannot be part of knowledge for

---

[44] Ibid., 398.
[45] Irigaray, "Plato's Hystera," 300. "The world is 'true' only insofar as it is engendered by Him alone, and related to Him alone."

Descartes, and knowledge is what he desires. It is ironic, then, that several early modern Christians took up various degrees of Cartesian epistemology (see Faber, "The sense of peace: a para-doxology of divine multiplicity," 46). The abundant, incarnate knowledge of Christian traditions was flattened into a thin sliver of intellectual assent, reduced to a rational decision, diminished to a cognitive truth claim. Among some early modern authors, the embodied and communal elements of Christianity were seen as unnecessary and even embarrassing.

Third, the Logic of the One has been functionally embraced by much of academia in the modern West. Several of Descartes' key epistemological principles have been integrated into the warp and woof of Western academics. While postmodernists have questioned body/spirit dualisms and the Logic of the One in recent decades, the structures of many educational institutions still imply and underwrite Cartesian epistemology. From classroom disciplines that imply separation between body and mind to goals of observational objectivity to tenure standards that focus on single-author research, Western academia is deeply Cartesian. When Irigaray describes the Logic of the One—the theoretical "orthodoxy of the One" in relation to which *Polydoxy* positions itself—she points towards academia as the disciplinary structure that enforces orthodoxy. The professor systematically blinds students to multiple ways of knowing until only one kind of truth remains, a truth which is deemed certain and stable.[46] Students thus initiated forget that they are turning cartwheels to see this way, forget they have been blinded, and accept the limited vision left them as self-evident truth.[47]

It is important to note the disciplinary role of academic theology. The ways in which theoretical orthodoxy have been taken up in Christian theology are not unrelated to the movement of the work of theology from the monastery or religious community into the university. In much of the modern West, what counts as Christian theology has been books written by academics trained in disembodied epistemology. This has never been all there is to Christian thought or conversation about God. Many Christian ways of knowing—singing, dancing, shouting, eating, kneeling, praying—are not amenable to Cartesian forms of investigation. They are hard to parse in the grammar of academia.

The authors of the essays in *Polydoxy* are performing constructive theology in a distinctive mode, in relation to a particular form of orthodoxy—theoretical orthodoxy in a modern, academic tone. This is the orthodoxy questioned in *Polydoxy: Theology of Multiplicity and Relation*. It is also the form of orthodoxy in which the authors and the readers of this text have been trained. Perhaps it is always true that the orthodoxy we strive against is the one that strikes closest to home; the bonds we strain against are on our own wrists.

---

[46] See Irigaray, "Plato's Hystera," 284–85, 305–306, 314.
[47] Ibid., 296, 305.

The theoretical and academic orthodoxy of the One cannot appreciate or account for the embodied, communal, and multiple realities of Christianity. Of course a group of constructive theologians who are attentive to these realities will perform theology in relation to this orthodoxy! The fires of Descartes, Fox, and Pascal (along with the theological epistemologies I have used these fires to represent) were each shaped and colored by the particular orthodoxies that impinged upon them. In much the same manner, the theological epistemology these authors are performing—the fire they kindle—is shaped and colored by the specific orthodoxy that impinges upon constructive, academic theologians who care deeply about the embodied, communal, and multiple realities of Christianity.

However, performing polydoxy in relationship to this singular orthodoxy reproduces the Logic of the One. Focusing on a singular orthodoxy—an orthodoxy of singularity—inhibits the multiplicity of polydoxy. The critique mirrors, repeats, and re-inscribes what is criticized. To a certain degree, this is unavoidable. Irigaray describes this difficulty as similar to being inside a concave mirror or a shiny, metal speculum. Our best attempts at doing something radically new and different will only reflect the light of the Sun, reproduce the Logic of the One. While we can only mirror the One, we can attempt to rebel in our reflecting, to enact a mimetic performance that disrupts the system in which we still participate.[48] With this in mind, the charge that the *Polydoxy* authors reflected the Logic of the One supports Irigaray's analysis.

Irigaray's writings attempt to evade singularity. Consider her description of the fire within her retelling of Plato's myth of the cave. Prisoners, shackled and facing the wall, see shadows of effigies projected by the light of the fire. One prisoner is unchained and taken to face the glaring brightness of the fire directly. This is the first step on the path towards the Sun, the first step in the prisoner's progressive blinding. The fire is ambiguous and multivalent. It can be understood as part of the Logic of the One, the Sun writ small for beginners, similar to the reading of Descartes' stove that I have offered here. Or Irigaray's fire can be understood as a different light, representing more multiple, communal, embodied ways of knowing. The prisoner must learn to forget this fire in order to participate in the heliocentric glory of the One. This take on Irigaray's fire looks more like those that warmed Fox and Pascal.

The various authors of *Polydoxy: Theology of Multiplicity and Relation* strive to value the multiple fires—the many ways of knowing—within diverse Christian traditions, while kindling their own. However, their efforts are limited by the fairly singular take on what constitutes orthodoxy. While Irigaray's brilliant analysis of the Logic of the One is an illuminating metanarrative, one of its primary purposes is to critique the application of illuminating metanarratives. Reading all orthodoxies through the lens of

---

[48] Regarding mimicry, see ibid., 307, 344.

Irigaray's critique re-inscribes the Logic of the Same that she protests. Furthermore, this pattern belies the relationality that polydoxy emphasizes. The blazing epistemologies of Descartes, Fox, and Pascal each came to be in relation to specific boundary-marking orthodoxies. Perhaps, then, the continuing development of polydoxy might require attending to the specific multiplicities of orthodoxy.

Modern Theology 30:3 July 2014
ISSN 0266-7177 (Print)
ISSN 1468-0025 (Online)

DOI: 10.1111/moth.12120

POLYHAIRESIS: ON POSTMODERN AND CHINESE FOLDS

CLAYTON CROCKETT

In this article, I am being self-consciously and deliberately pro-Choice. I am choosing to reflect on Colleen Hartung's provocative and bracing claim that "theology does not have to assume a God or divinity to be theological."[1] What does Hartung mean by this claim? This is the subject of my argument. The overall volume *Polydoxy: Theology of Multiplicity and Relation*, is an incredibly rich collection of texts and ideas. I cannot pretend to do justice to the scope of the book as a whole, but choose to focus more narrowly on a couple of the chapters. First of all, though, what does it mean to choose? Am I a free self-legislating rational sovereign subject, or have I been "chosen" to take on this particular paradoxical topic? Am I determined by fate, God, experience, bio-genetics, instinct or something else either totally or partially in my illusion of choice? Where is the freedom to choose? Who has it, and by what authority and for what ends?[2]

To insist on choice is to flirt with heresy. The etymology of heresy can be traced to the Greek word *hairesis*, which means to choose, and the implication is that such choice is in itself wrong and to be condemned. Orthodox

---

Clayton Crockett
Department of Philosophy and Religion, University of Central Arkansas, 201 Donaghey Avenue, Conway, AR 72035, USA
Email: claytonc@uca.edu

[1] Colleen Hartung, "Faith and Polydoxy in the Whirlwind," in Catherine Keller and Laurel Schneider, eds., *Polydoxy: Theology of Multiplicity of Religion* (New York: Routledge, 2010), 153. Subsequent references to *Polydoxy* will be cited internally according to author, title, and page number.

[2] See the complex and nuanced discussion of choice for Muslim women in Egypt by Saba Mahmood, *The Politics of Piety: The Islamic Revival and the Feminist Subject* (Princeton, NJ: Princeton University Press, 2005). Mahmood explains that women in the piety movement in contemporary Egypt do not conform to the liberal-humanist notions of free choice, but these women nevertheless still exercise choice and perform agency. She says that "as such, choice is understood not to be an expression of one's will but something one exercises in following the prescribed path to becoming a better Muslim" (85).

Christianity emerged precisely by rejecting Gnostic Christianity as heresy. Why did Orthodoxy reject gnosis? Who doesn't want knowledge or wisdom, especially the secret, salvific wisdom taught by Jesus? Orthodoxy determined that Jesus's teachings were for the many, not the few, and they organized the administration of churches under the authority of bishops, who were seen as successors of the original apostles. My argument here is not with the specific rejection of Gnosticism, which is largely understood in negative terms at least until the discovery of the extraordinary sources at Nag Hammadi, but rather with the association of wrong with choice, the idea of choosing the faith as opposed to being subjected to it.

So I choose and therefore I am a heretic. I choose and it's necessarily the wrong choice, even if it's the right one, the orthodox one (but this is less obvious and much more subtle), because the problem is with choice itself, the presumption that one could choose faith. Do we choose our faith, or are we born with it? Part of the fantasy of Protestant Christianity lies with the presupposition that we are simply free to choose to be Christian or not, or even which kind of Christian we might be. On this account Protestant Christianity is a heresy, at least in its Arminianist varieties. But maybe choice is not so superficial. Maybe a choice, free or otherwise, has something abyssal or aporetic about it, to use juicy postmodern words. Can we disjoin choice from its place in a libertarian economy that values economic choice solely in terms of markets? Perhaps choice, like heresy, is multiple and possesses many folds.

Here I am choosing not only to dwell on Hartung's essay and question, but in addition and at the same time to pursue a quasi-Chinese fold, partly because Chinese cultures and traditions do not appear obviously religious, much less theological, at least in conventional terms. And yet for sake of the academic field of the comparative study of religion we are constrained to view Confucianism and Daoism as religions, at least in part.[3] Another reason I choose to think about China is due to the resurgence of Chinese economy, nationalism and culture. Many Westerners are forced to reckon with China today, in ways that were not apparent a few decades ago, including the Chinese Communist party's embrace of capitalism and China's extraordinary economic growth that, in turn, fuels American consumption. At the same time, China's enormous population, pollution, and energy needs means that we are facing serious limits to worldwide growth, so it's not simply a question of whether China can replace the United States as the global superpower in the near future.

An additional reason I want to think about China in this article is a choice (or is it a demand? Does the text place a demand on me, or am I free to engage

---

[3] On the modern construction of comparative world religions, which is not a neutral process, see Tomoko Masuzawa, *The Invention of World Religions: Or, How European Universalism was Preserved in the Language of Pluralism* (Chicago, IL: University of Chicago Press, 2005).

it, raise it up or set it aside?) to respond to Hyo-dong Lee's excellent chapter on the Great Ultimate in neo-Confucianism in the volume *Polydoxy: Theology of Multiplicity and Relation* (126–150), even if I ultimately pursue a more Daoist line. Finally, I want to choose to return to or remain in the whirlwind, the secular whirlwind of Hartung's that is nonetheless profoundly theological, where "no news is good news." No news is good news because the Dao that can be named is not the true name; at least that's how I choose to see it.

In the Beginning was Dao

So why did Bodhidharma, the legendary founder of Chan Buddhism, come to China from India? This is not simply a scholarly question, and if it is it is literally unanswerable, because we have no historical evidence that Bodhidharma ever existed. There is an imaginary quality to Bodhidharma's passage from India to China that mirrors the trajectory of Buddhism. In any case, we do know that Buddhism (although probably not Chan, which in all likelihood originated in China) spread from India to China sometime around the beginning of the Common Era. Two very interesting elements of this story are first, that due to a misunderstanding about the chronology of textual composition, Chinese scholars beginning in the first or second century CE translated and adopted Mahayana sutras rather than earlier Nikaya sutras such as the Pali Canon. Second, the introduction and later important influence of Buddhism as an explicitly developed religious tradition in China served to organize and discipline Confucianism and Daoism as competing religious traditions themselves, even though this process made them both appear very different from their original forms. Originally, Confucianism and Daoism were more akin to political and/or moral philosophies, or at most practical wisdom traditions, but they were neither distinct from nor organized in terms of religious practices of monasticism and worship characteristic of typical religious orientations to the supernatural, the soul or the afterlife.[4]

I am interested in Buddhism's entry into China partly because this process is repeated differently in the modern period, where British colonialism applies a Christian religious typology to both Indian and Chinese polydox faiths and practices. I do not choose to retell this story, but just mention it to indicate that the modern colonial imposition and application of religion to non-Western and non-modern peoples is a fraught and terrible encounter, whose trauma we are still living.[5] At the same time, the experience of Buddhism in China serves as a reminder that the modern Christian mission was not the first such inter-religious encounter. What is interesting is how

---

[4] See Jeeloo Liu, *An Introduction to Chinese Philosophy: From Ancient Philosophy to Chinese Buddhism* (London: Wiley-Blackwell, 2006).

[5] See, for just one example, David Chidester, *Savage Systems: Colonialism and Comparative Religions in Southern Africa* (Charlottesville, VA: University of Virginia Press, 1996).

Chinese "religions" are subjected to two very distinct encounters (first with Buddhism and later with Christianity) that attempt to shape Chinese traditions into a form of religious orthodoxy, even as Chinese faiths continue to resist this appellation.

There is Great Disorder under Heaven . . . the Situation is Excellent—
Mao Zedong

When great troubles occur, as reflective creatures we naturally ask why? Why am I or why are my loved ones hungry, sick, impoverished, stricken, raped, or murdered? How does the world make sense given pain and suffering, particularly in sudden, overwhelming and catastrophic terms? Where is God in the camps, the secret torture prisons, the tornado, the earthquake or the tsunami? If we are groups of human beings who rely solely on oral language, scholars explain that we tend to anthropomorphize and personalize impersonal forces, whether meteorological, cosmic, natural or social, and we often call them gods or spirits in attributing to them an almost undeniable intentionality. When humans mastered the complex revolutionary technology of writing scrolls and books, we came to imagine that the divine also chooses to reveal itself to humanity by means of written texts, and this process canalized religious experience along textual lines. The consolidation of writing and books leads to a presupposition that a single Book has a single author, so there gradually emerged the thesis that only one God exists, rather than many. During the course of European modernity, some theorists of religion remain impressed with monotheism, which abstracts and removes God from the realm of ordinary human experience. As modern scientific understanding proceeds, however, we have naturalistic and disenchanted explanations for why disasters happen: people get sick due to micro-organisms, earthquakes occur due to moving tectonic plates, and wars are started by greedy and power-hungry humans, not bored gods and goddesses with nothing better to do. For some people who choose to remain religious believers, God functions providentially as a guarantee that someone or something is in charge; there is an explanation for why everything happens, including bad happenings. Ultimately, there will be a life after death where deserts will match deservers, which does not seem to take place in this life. Some other humans, impressed by the explanatory power of modern science, or deeply sensitive to the tragic nature of human life, choose to slough off this belief in a providential God. Here is a kind of superficial opposition between theism and atheism, which may be challenged by more sophisticated theological discourses, including the ones discussed and deployed in *Polydoxy*.

I read process theology as a serious, sensitive, honest and courageous effort to retrieve some semblance of God for human experience in the modern world, spurred by Whitehead's impressive and ambitious synthesis in *Process and Reality*. I am not a process theologian, I have to confess, and this is by choice, whatever that means. Various forms of post-colonial and libera-tion theological modes of inquiry seek to retain Biblical narratives and adapt them to struggles for justice and ecological sanity in a post-patriarchal context. I am not a liberation theologian either, by choice. This is not to say that I do not respect or admire these vital forms of theological thinking and practice today, from which I have learned much and been enriched, in mul-tiple ways. I confess that I am a postmodern theologian, or a thinker who is shaped by contemporary Continental philosophy of religion, for better and for worse. And I do not know whether or not this was solely my choice, but I have chosen and made my peace with it, despite all the mischief that postmodern theory has done and continues to do. I have never been particu-larly attracted to any form of Christian orthodoxy, at least since I lost my faith in high school, so the distance from orthodoxy taken in *Polydoxy: Theology of Multiplicity and Relation* resonates strongly with me. Furthermore, I appreci-ate very much the serious, sustained and responsible engagement with non-Christian and non-Western forms of religion and theology, which presses beyond any simple model of inter-religious dialogue. Religious dialogue often presumes and takes place under the sign of identity rather than multi-plicity, including the lack of appreciation of the irreducible multiplicity of one's own religious tradition.

Colleen Hartung's chapter, "Faith and Polydoxy in the Whirlwind," takes this impressive collection of texts marked by various elements of process, liberation and postmodern theology, to an important limit. At the opening of her essay, Hartung recalls a powerful tornado that raged across Nebraska in 1975 while she was in her first year in college (Hartung, "Faith and Polydoxy in the Whirlwind," 151–152). I can resonate with her experience because tornadoes bombarded Arkansas in spring 2011, including one that killed six people in Vilonia, Arkansas, about fifteen miles from where I live and work. Tornadoes also devastated Alabama and killed dozens of people, and finally the most brutal storm of the season killed over a hundred people in Joplin, Missouri in May 2011, laying much of the town to waste. In her case, Hartung explains that while she was unhurt, the city of Omaha was cut off and there was no way to communicate with her parents. She reflects upon her mother's statement that her family took the absence of specific news as an encouraging sign that she was not dead or seriously injured. Hartung says that this taking of no news, which could have been anguishing in its uncertainty, for good news, was "an extraordinary act of faith considering that it would have been five years that June since my brother had died of leukemia" (Hartung, "Faith and Polydoxy in the Whirlwind," 152). A very similar act of faith consists in telling your children they will be fine as the sirens go off while you huddle with your family in the bathtub because the water table is too high for homes in central Arkansas to have basements. This faith on the part of her mother, that "no news was good news," expresses the polydoxy she articulates in theoretical terms, using Derrida and Caputo.

Faith can take place in the absence of God, without God. Hartung evokes the *sans* that pervades Derrida's work, partly as expressed so powerfully and eloquently by John D. Caputo. She says that "Derrida's pursuit of the *sans* provides language that makes a faith without God, that is open to what is wholly other, theoretically intelligible" (Hartung, "Faith and Polydoxy in the Whirlwind," 153). It seems to me that religious language *requires* God to be absent, or at least distant, in order to make a faith. Otherwise it wouldn't be faith. That does not mean that God does not or cannot exist, but God cannot collapse the spacing required for faith, and some faiths work with God while other faiths may authentically take place without God. Or at least, we could choose to value these faiths without God as authentic, rather than inauthentic, as lacking, or as being simply and neatly non-religious.

Hartung raises the stakes even further when she admits that she raids three contemporary theologians for three distinct insights that she then dislocates from the rest of their theological edifices, and then assimilates to her own theological vision, which is a theology without God (Hartung, "Faith and Polydoxy in the Whirlwind," 153). What is more, she chooses to elaborate her themes of blindness, embrace and courage, by way of an appropriation of and separation from three of the most creative and important theologians working and writing today, and not only that, from three theologians whose chapters are also included in the book *Polydoxy*, two of whom are the very editors who presumably enfranchised, selected, and approved Hartung's own work to be included within it! These two theologians of course are Laurel Schneider and Catherine Keller, and their theologies should be absolutely required reading for anyone in the English-speaking world who chooses to think theologically today. The third is Mayra Rivera, whose rehabilitation of glory in liberationist theological terms in her chapter in the volume is itself stunning, as are many of the other chapters. But I choose to stay with Hartung, and her appropriation of Schneider, Rivera, and Keller.

Schneider is a theologian of multiplicity, and dislodging the logic of the One allows her to see divinity in its manifestation as multiplicity. Hartung claims that for Schneider, "to face and to see the fragile is to realize divine occurrence as incarnation again and again" (Hartung, "Faith and Polydoxy in the Whirlwind," 154). By contrast, Hartung remains faithful to the blindness inherent in her mother's faith and in Derrida's thought that paradoxically sustains faith. According to Hartung, "Schneider's emphasis on presence and on seeing . . . considered from a Derridean perspective, might collapse this space between believing and seeing that Derrida attempts to keep open as a way of holding at bay a totalizing foreclosure that a too optical metaphysics of presence effects" (Hartung, "Faith and Polydoxy in the Whirlwind," 155). If Hartung is correct, then Schneider twists free of the logic and metaphysics of the One, but perhaps her theology is still too entranced with a metaphorics and metaphysics of vision. Despite this distancing from Schneider's affinity for seeing, Hartung celebrates Schneider's foregrounding of ambiguity in bodies and in faith.

From Rivera, Hartung takes the phenomenality of touch or even embrace. Faith is a risky embrace of what is uncertain and unknown. But Rivera chooses to hold onto a transcendence in which she anchors her understanding of faith as touch. As for Hartung, she chooses instead to remain faithful to the faith of her parents after the death of her brother, who "let go of the name of God and yet in that release realized a faith that could and would, again and again, turn toward an unthinkable, unspeakable, ungraspable possibility—the death of a child" (Hartung, "Faith and Polydoxy in the Whirlwind," 158). The death of one's child would seem to be one of the most faith-shattering events that could ever occur. Rivera wants to limit Derridean deconstruction by tracing its originary source to divine transcendence on the other side of *différance*. Hartung, however, wants to remain with *différance* and its indeterminacy all the way. This is a cryptic move, just as the saying "no news is good news" is a cryptic saying, but "perhaps it could be read as a disclosure, as an opening that might make a space for love" (Hartung, "Faith and Polydoxy in the Whirlwind," 159). Do we need God or divinity to make love with and as bodies, or does the heaviness of God's transcendence weigh love down? Hartung uses the image of a surrender of arms; she evokes the notion of giving up our arms and embracing life without the conceptual tools we generally employ to keep it in check. "Here the surrender of arms is an embrace," she says, "without the benefit of technological or religious good news" (Hartung, "Faith and Polydoxy in the Whirlwind," 159). Technological and religious arms are deployed to overdetermine life, to make it make sense, to make it appear good, to instrumentalize our experience and protect us from the uncertainty that makes living worthwhile. But these arms ward off "the possibility of the coming of the new" (Hartung, "Faith and Polydoxy in the Whirlwind," 159).

With Keller, finally, Hartung is more tentative than with Rivera or Schneider. Hartung appreciates and appropriates Keller's courage in the face of the deep, which is also the tehomic fury of the whirlwind. The only thing she lets go of that Keller does not is the issue with which Hartung begins this section of encounters: the name of God. Hartung confesses, "for me, the tehomic rhythm of life has washed away any name that would underwrite faith with a destinal assurance. Yet this has not left me faithless" (Hartung, "Faith and Polydoxy in the Whirlwind," 160). Here there is a tension, because while Keller does not give up the name of God, she also does not provide it any destinal assurance. For Keller, any discussion of God concerns "a becoming God, who inasmuch as we have language for it/them/her/him, is at a minimum an irreducible effect of language."[6] Furthermore, although

---

[6] Catherine Keller, *Face of the Deep: A Theology of Becoming* (London: Routledge, 2003), 182.

Hartung appeals to Derrida and Caputo for her notion of faith without God, at least Caputo if not Derrida holds onto the name of God, but also in a way that would not guarantee or underwrite faith in any substantial way. Derrida is more complicated, because for him he both saves and gives up the name of God, and the *sans* is not a simple without, but always both a with and a without. This is a paradox, but then so is faith.

But the real issue here concerns Hartung's provocative claim, which she expresses in relation to both Schneider and Keller (and Rivera more implicitly): "in its polydoxy, theology risks a consideration of faith without the name of God" (Hartung, "Faith and Polydoxy in the Whirlwind," 161). Now, the idea of a theology without God is not entirely new, and there is a tradition of American "death of God" theology that goes back to the 1960s. Many theologians and non-theologians are all too happy to proclaim and even to celebrate the *death* of this strange death-of-God theology.[7] And, to be sure, it certainly was not polydox enough in its original incarnation, even if it was not orthodox in any recognizable way. Nevertheless, something like the death of God understood as the distance between the reality of God and theological discourse about God persists, and perhaps even haunts contemporary theological discourse, including that of Caputo and Keller. Hartung quotes Keller as raising the relevant question: "What would theology be *without* theos?" (Hartung, "Faith and Polydoxy in the Whirlwind," 161). Keller does not answer this question, according to Hartung, but Hartung does suggest, with Derrida, that alternative theological beginnings without God could resonate "with a faithful Derridean deconstructive posture that courageously turns toward the unforeseeable" (Hartung, "Faith and Polydoxy in the Whirlwind," 162). The passion of a faith without God no longer knows to whom or what to pray. One of the effects of moving between determinate faiths is a wearing away of any pure, authentic or determinate lineage, and Hartung evokes this experience both for herself and for Derrida. She says that Derrida's "is not a legacy of faith inscribed in a determinable lineage that might be Christian or Jewish or democratic. Rather this inheritance is a plea . . ." (Hartung, "Faith and Polydoxy in the Whirlwind," 162). So the tehomic rhythms that ebb and flow may wear down the sharp edges of determinate lineages, and the lines may blur such that we do not know not only to whom we pray but who we are when we pray or plead. And this is a complex inheritance, which is incarnated in Hartung's mother and her particular faith.

For Hartung, her mother's theology, encapsulated in the phrase "no news is good news," "resists gestures of faith that make light of a darkness, a blindness, and a grief that is the undoing of oneself and of the world over and over again" (Hartung, "Faith and Polydoxy in the Whirlwind," 162). We do not often get good news, but sometimes no news is the best news we could

---

[7] See John D. Caputo and Gianni Vattimo, *After the Death of God*, Jeffrey W. Robbins (ed) (New York: Columbia University Press, 2007).

ever receive, and most of the time we have no idea how fortunate we are not to get news of disaster, illness, or the death of a loved one. What Hartung performs in this extraordinary essay is an existential theology that is not conceptually impoverished, but one that finds a way to honor both Derrida and her mother by threading her theology through the eye of the needle of three polydox theologians and stitching together something both refreshing and common. This faith of Hartung's mother as elaborated through Derrida "insinuates rather than claims. It holds on for dear life," caught up amidst the whirlwind (Hartung, "Faith and Polydoxy in the Whirlwind," 163).

Hold on.

For God so Loved the World, he Sent his Other Son Hong, Jesus's Younger Brother, to China. In the Failed Taiping Rebellion against the Manchu Rulers, Approximately Twenty Million People Died[8]

In the essay that immediately precedes Hartung's in the book, Hyo-dong Lee wrestles with the Neo-Confucian notion of ultimate reality, or the Great Ultimate. The Great Ultimate is characterized by the phrase, "Empty and tranquil, and without any sign, and yet all things are luxuriously present," and this phrase also serves as the title of Lee's essay. Lee explicates this phrase in the work of Zhu Xi and Yi Hwang, as a way of providing "helpful resources for Christian theology in exploring the kind of Spirit-centered trinitarian panentheism that does justice to both the unifying and pluralizing motif found in the biblical pneumatological tradition" (Lee, " 'Empty and tranquil, and without any sign, and yet all things are already luxuriantly present': a comparative theological reflection on the manifold Spirit," 127). I do not want to resist this comparison to Christianity, but I prefer to linger with the Neo-Confucian resonances of Lee's discussion. Neo-Confucianism names the result of a metaphysical formulation that would be adequate not only to classical Confucianism, but also the ideas and practices of Buddhism and Daoism in China.

As Lee explains, the Great Ultimate refers to the "ultimate structure or 'logic' of everything that is" (Lee, " 'Empty and tranquil,'" 128). The Great Ultimate "points to the fact that, while reality is at root differentiated and plural, that plurality consists of a harmoniously interrelated and unified multiplicity, not sheer, unrelated multiplicity" (Lee, "Empty and tranquil," 128). How is reality differentiated? One major way to perceive existence in Chinese terms is to view it as the inter-relationship of two opposite but complementary forces, *yin* and *yang*. Yin and yang work together to generate the five elements or agents: wood, fire, earth, metal and water. What is the nature of these forces? Yin and yang are understood in terms of *qi*, which

---

[8] See Jonathan D. Spence, *God's Chinese Son: The Taiping Heavenly Kingdom of Hong Xiuquan* (New York: W. W. Norton and Co., 1996).

means a kind of psychophysical energy. That is, the energy or force that qi is does not make a hard and fast distinction between material energy and psychic or spiritual energy. The problem with qi is that from the standpoint of the Great Ultimate, it appears to be too formless and irrational. This is the reason that the greatest and most influential Neo-Confucian thinker, Zhu Xi, develops the notion of *li*, or principle, as a counter-balance to qi. Qi as the encapsulation of *dao*, the way that things manifest, interact, and change, must be correlated to and perhaps even subordinated to li. Lee says that "the dominant philosophical tradition of Neo-Confucianism represented by Zhu Xi posits principle [li] as the metaphysical ultimate, which is logically and ontologically prior to psychophysical energy [qi,] and upon which the cosmic creativity of the latter is dependent" (Lee, "Empty and tranquil," 129).

For Zhu Xi and therefore for most Neo-Confucians, li as principle (not to be confused with the original Confucian virtue of propriety, which is also transliterated as li) provides the structuring pattern for qi that harmonizes it and renders it into a component of the Great Ultimate. The Great Ultimate is the harmonious inter-relationship of li and qi, and furthermore, according to Zhu Xi, "the Great Ultimate is everywhere, in every single being or process in the world" (Lee, "Empty and tranquil," p. 129). Although the Great Ultimate is composed of li and qi, then, Zhu Xi clearly privileges li and makes qi subordinate to the principle of li. By itself li is understood as quiescent and still, a potential and substantial One. Li needs qi to provide the dynamic psychophysical energy to actualize li as a process or operating function. "In Zhu Xi's account," Lee explains, "principle as substance is the indeterminate and quiescent One. It is only when principle is activated, when it is united with psychophysical energy, that multiplicity is introduced into it" (Lee, "Empty and tranquil," 131).

Lee sees a problem in this denial of function and multiplicity to the overarching principle of the Great Ultimate. He therefore turns to another, lesser-known Neo-Confucian, Yi Hwang, for a better account of principle. According to Lee, Neo-Confucian morality is concerned with the cultivation of *shen*, which can be translated as spirit, or in more conventional ethical terms, "heart-mind." The Chinese language does not make a clear distinction between what we call heart in emotional terms and the intellectual mind. The goal of Neo-Confucianism (as of Daoism) is to cultivate and create shen as spirit, but shen is also understood as a rarefied form of qi, or psychophysical energy. In Yi Hwang's terms, the fact that Zhu Xi denies any "independent dynamism to the metaphysical ultimate, or principle, presents a serious challenge to the moral agency of the heart-mind" (Lee, "Empty and tranquil," 135). How can heart-mind acquire li if li cannot function without the dynamism of qi, which is also heart-mind but in a potentially impure form? Yi Hwang wants principle to have a dynamic function within itself, without requiring the external agency of qi, in order to produce yang and yin, which then produce the manifold. In this way, the Great Ultimate becomes an intrinsic and dynamic force of moral agency. For Lee, Yi Hwang's formulation of li as "principle's capacity to be an active and effective source of unity and harmony in the world" restores a kind of multiplicity to the heart of principle. In addition, Lee claims that "Yi Hwang's affirmation of principle's own dynamism opens up a path toward something akin to panentheism within the rubrics of the Neo-Confucian worldview" (Lee, "Empty and tranquil," 137).

So multiplicity and dynamicity work at the level of li, but only by appropriating and restraining the intrinsic force of qi. According to Lee, by following Yi Hwang's attribution of dynamic functionality to li, we can think of the Great Ultimate as a moral agent of heart-mind and ultimately as Spirit. Spirit, like the Great Ultimate, is both one and many, unifying and disseminating, yang and yin. But most importantly, a Neo-Confucian understanding of Spirit following Yi Hwang is "panentheistic in the sense that, while principle is a dynamic creativity logically and ontologically prior to psychophysical energy, this creativity is never active outside of that to which it has given birth" (Lee, "Empty and tranquil," 139). Spirit has it both ways; it gets to be sovereign and apart from psychophysical energy in order to consolidate its own priority and power, *and* it gets to interact and manifest itself by means of its own dynamic agency by expressing itself in terms of psychophysical energy. There is no substance dualism, but there is a hierarchy of spirit in this understanding of li, and one that could be seen as a further denigration of the function of qi, which could do something dynamic that li could not in Zhu Xi's philosophy. If Lee is right to see the direct application of his model of Neo-Confucian spirit to the process theological model of panentheism, then this raises a question about the adequacy of panentheism more broadly. Does God as Great Ultimate reserve the powers of both substantiality and functionality, and deny any intrinsic functionality and substantiality to material creation, even as the material world is a functional multiplicity that in some ways operates independently of God without thereby degenerating into a dualistic ontology? Does the designation of material force and energy as the primordial nature of God in Whitehead's terms function to arrogate the dynamic energizing forces of reality to the principle of God? And finally, does the priority of principle, understood in the West more generally as *logos*, then re-instantiate the logic of the One that polydoxy attempts to evade?

Perhaps Lee's Neo-Confucian panentheism is not "orthodox" process panentheism. But then to defend a more correct, Christian version of panentheism would undermine the polydoxy that at least some forms of process theology seek to promote, here in this book most of all. Furthermore, Lee himself recognizes the problem at the end of his essay, even if he does not flesh it out. Lee admits that one drawback of his Neo-Confucian understanding of spirit is that "in its present formulation, mainly drawing on Zhu Xi and Yi Hwang, it does not challenge the dominant Neo-Confucian refusal to recognize the existence of an intrinsically unifying and harmonizing dynamic in psychophysical energy" (Lee, "Empty and tranquil," 142). He suggests that a more interdependent model of the relation between li and qi "would give us a doctrine of the manifold Spirit that readily affirms the real plurality of harmonious socio-ecological configurations emerging from our embodied ... and therefore multiple agencies" (Lee, "Empty and tranquil," 142). The question, then, is how this model and vision of manifold Spirit would differ from Lee's original presentation of Zhu Xi's understanding of the harmonious interplay of principle and energy.

What if we went in this third direction intimated but not developed by Lee? On the one hand, there is the thinking about li as substance and qi as function in the "orthodox" Neo-Confucianism of Zhu Xi. On the other hand, there is the alternative option that Lee presents, of thinking about li as itself possessing a dynamic functional quality that it then shares with and into qi as in Yi Hwang (and perhaps also panentheistic Neo-Confucianism). What would it mean, however, to think about qi or psychophysical energy as possessing its own li, rather than requiring li to give it reason or to operationalize it?

In order to think about energy's intrinsic dynamism and unifying harmony, I want to turn to a newer Western scientific understanding of thermodynamics. For most people, thermodynamics indicates the absolute priority of its first two laws; the first, which refers to the conservation of energy, and the second, which states that in any closed system at equilibrium, the organization of energy tends toward disorder, or entropy. In this traditional view, energy, while in principle absolute, in practice breaks down and provides less and less useful work the more thoroughly it can be exploited. If energy tends toward a maximum of disorder, then it appears to be the precise opposite of li, or ordered principle.

But a newer understanding of nonequilibrium thermodynamics has emerged over the past few decades, which understands energy more in terms of gradient reduction than in terms of entropy. As Eric D. Schneider and Dorion Sagan explain in their book *Into the Cool*, energy flow through systems that are not at equilibrium works to reduce gradient differentials in the most efficient way possible. They rewrite the famous Second Law of thermodynamics as: "Nature Abhors a Gradient."[9] Gradients can be temperature differentials, pressure differentials, or other physical differentials, and what entropy in nature means is that these gradients tend to be reduced as quickly as possible. In most cases, this gradient reduction produces disorder, but in highly specific situations with open systems that are not at equilibrium, the flow of energy organizes a system into a gradient reducing machine that persists as long as the energy flows through it. As an example, consider a "storm in a bottle." If you take two one-liter bottles and fill one of the bottles

---

[9] Eric D. Schneider and Dorion Sagan, *Into the Cool: Energy Flow, Thermodynamics, and Life* (Chicago, IL: University of Chicago Press, 2006), 77.

with water and join them at the necks, and then turn it over, the water will fall due to gravity from one bottle into the other, but at a very slow rate. But if you twist the bottle to organize a tornado-like motion, this system persists until the bottle is emptied, and the bottle empties much more quickly than a bottle that lacks such organization.[10]

Although many of the scientific ideas and principles that make up this nonequilibrium thermodynamics have been developed over the course of the twentieth century, Schneider and Sagan synthesize the disparate results and explain the overall significance of this new science. They examine not only physical systems, but also living systems in light of energy flow and nonequilibrium thermodynamics. One important implication is that they show that entropy and thermodynamics do not oppose or work against the organization of life in evolutionary terms, but in fact evolution is a result of entropy as gradient reduction itself, because it relies upon more efficient ways to degrade gradients and the development of processes that retard the decay of the system in general. Here entropy as gradient reduction offers new ways to think about energy or qi as dynamic and self-organizing, that is, as producing principles of li out of its own intrinsic work. If Schneider and Sagan are correct, we do not require the external imposition of order on a system that naturally tends towards disorder. Entropy as gradient production is itself the production of order under specific conditions.

What is even more fascinating is that physical systems that reduce gradients by self-organizing when subjected to flows of energy seem to exhibit a kind of memory. In a discussion of Taylor vortices, which refers to the rotation of cylinders inside other cylinders that are filled with fluid, Schneider and Sagan point out that "retardation or lagging (called hysteresis) occurs in the development of Taylor flow patterns."[11] This hysteresis functions as an implicit memory of past states, such that without the knowledge of the previous history of the system you cannot predict how or when such cycles will reduce gradients and achieve states of equilibrium. The complexity of a nonequilibrium system exhibits a patternicity that "remembers" previous states because the fact of having been in that state affects the system's future state, which cannot be predicted without knowledge of these past states.

Energy flow organizes living and nonliving systems by allowing for the reduction of gradient differentials in complex and highly efficient ways. Energy flow produces patterns or principles out of its intrinsic dynamic workings, rather than relying on external principles to organize and legislate it. Here is a contemporary example of qi that is not subordinated to li. We could follow Chinese thought more broadly and refuse to institute a dualism between spiritual and material energy. What if what we call spirit (shen) is a refined and highly specific form of qi, but qi is itself neither strictly material

---

[10] See ibid., 132.
[11] Ibid., 129.

nor solely spiritual? In fact, qi is both material energy and spiritual energy, which is one reason that it is such a provocative concept, even possibly a theological concept.

What does it mean to say that qi is a theological concept? In light of Hartung's notion of a theology without divinity, perhaps a theology that thinks with and about qi could be potentially significant. I have read Lee's essay appreciatively, but also in order to liberate a notion of qi beyond its subordination to or appropriation by li. This might be a more Daoist reading than Lee's Neo-Confucian interpretation of the Great Ultimate. If so, how is qi connected to dao, and how are qi and dao related to the quasi-theological slogan of Hartung's mother: "no news is good news"? I do not have any sort of final answer, but in order to reflect a little further, and by way of conclusion, I would like to briefly consider the *Daode jing*.

Qi emerges as a more neo-Daoist and neo-Confucian notion, although we can project it back into the *Daode jing* as a name for what yin and yang express, as the characterization of the energies that manifest dao. Dao can be understood as the source of everything, the rhythm of their interaction, or the way of existence's manifestation. Dao could be seen in more properly Daoist terms anachronistically as a name for the Great Ultimate, or it could simply be seen as nature.

The famous first chapter of the *Daode jing* reads (in a popular translation):

The Dao that can be told is not the eternal Dao.
The name that can be named is not the eternal name.
The nameless is the beginning of heaven and earth.
The named is the mother of ten thousand things.
Ever desireless, one can see the mystery.
Ever desiring, one sees the manifestations.
These two spring from the same source, but differ in name; this appears as darkness.
Darkness within darkness.
The gate to all mystery.[12]

This passage has been read and interpreted in myriad ways, and part of its richness is its resistance to any easy interpretation or signification, even as it lends itself easily to a reader's understanding, and can function similarly to a Rorschach test. My own understanding focuses on the couplets, which distinguish two different perspectives without separating them into a dualistic opposition. For example, the nameless is the source of heaven and earth, while the named gives rise to countless phenomena, the "ten thousand

---

[12] Lao Tsu, *Tao Te Ching*, Gia-Fu Feng and Jane English (trans), (New York: Random House, 1989), 3.

things." These two perspectives are distinguished but not opposed, just like yin and yang. The key is the third-to-last line, which explains that that which can be seen and said and that which is "mystery" both proceed from the same source, but differ in name. That is, the difference between the two perspectives is the difference between the same phenomena from the standpoint of names and the standpoint of what cannot be named. This paradoxical tension "appears as darkness," but this "darkness within darkness" is nevertheless the gate to unlocking the mystery.

The yin is literally represented as black or darkness, which is why the yin is the gateway to the dao in Daoism. Yin is the way to understand, value and appreciate the way that dao works and manifests, as opposed to the yang, which leads people to misunderstand the true nature of dao. Yin's work as darkness within darkness unworks or undoes our natural way of seeing things, and this un-working appears as a kind of inaction or non-action, called wu-wei. Wu-wei means actionless activity, which involves doing nothing, and doing nothing paradoxically accomplishes more than doing something or especially doing a lot of things. It's not literally doing nothing; it's the idea of economy or the principle of least and most efficient action: "a great tailor cuts little."[13]

The more we do, the more we have to do. This is a principle of accumulation, where we keep acquiring more and more actions and therefore things, qualities, or characteristics. Human existence on earth is reaching the limits of this more and more, and we are starting to realize that we will have to do and have and be less if we want to continue to survive on this planet.

> Less and less is done
> Until non-action is achieved.
> When nothing is done, nothing is left undone.[14]

We need to learn how to do nothing, which is strictly speaking impossible, but that makes it no less necessary. Qi is conserved, always, but in its manifestation it seeks the most efficient means of gradient reduction. We need to conserve qi, and follow the lead of dao, and learn to view entropy more in terms of gradient reduction or in more spiritual terms as creative transformation, or zaohua. This is a more material manifestation of spirit, but it can also be seen as a spiritual manifestation of matter. In regard to the spirit/matter distinction, mapped onto a division between yang and yin, yin would be matter and yang would be spirit. In proper Daoist terms, the yin or material is the gateway to dao, rather than the more obvious and straightforward path of spirit. And ultimately, spirit or shen would be seen as a manifestation of qi, as we have already seen.

---

[13] Ibid., 30.
[14] Ibid., 50.

The lack of a proper name, or the gap between a substantializing name and the dynamic process to which it refers, is auspicious. If the name truly names a thing, then it blocks all movement, transformation and change. The dao that can be named as dao is not the true dao. The name that is named is not the eternal name. This is why Meister Eckhart says in one of his sermons, "I pray God to rid me of God," which is one of Caputo's favorite prayers.[15] Here is another register of meaning for the phrase, "no news is good news." The good news is that news is no news, or this news cannot be fully and finally named and grasped and even proclaimed as news. There is always more to it, which is good. The liberation of theological thinking and living even from the name of God can be good news, not simply negative.

The first paragraph of chapter 25 of the *Daode jing* reads:

> Something mysteriously formed,
> Born before heaven and earth.
> In the silence and the void,
> Standing alone and unchanging,
> Ever present and in motion.
> Perhaps it is the mother of ten thousand things.
> I do not know its name
> Call it Dao.
> For lack of a better word, I call it great.[16]

No news is good news. For lack of better words, I call it dao (source). I call it qi (energy). I call it shen (spirit). Here is an asymmetrical polydoxic trinitarian (un-)naming, in the mode of an English transliteration of Chinese, a sort of postmodern polyglossia. This is the body of my thinking, which results from a mani-folded choice, that emerges out of the depths of an experimental and open-ended polyhairesis. You can call it God, if you choose.

---

[15] John D. Caputo, *On Religion* (London: Routledge, 2001), 93.
[16] Ibid., 27.

Modern Theology 30:3 July 2014
ISSN 0266-7177 (Print)
ISSN 1468-0025 (Online)

DOI: 10.1111/moth.12121

THE LOGIC OF ORIGIN AND THE PARADOXES OF LANGUAGE: A THEOLOGICAL EXPERIMENT

LINN MARIE TONSTAD

A polydox theology starts from the insight, as Catherine Keller and Laurel Schneider state in the introduction to *Polydoxy: Theology of Multiplicity and Relation*, that *"multiplicity itself* has become theology's resource," unexpectedly and "miraculously" transformed from "liability" to "friend."[1] Polydoxy values "multiplicity, the evolutionary uncertainty it unfolds, and the relationality that it implies" in its understanding of divinity as well as in the resources it uses to interpret that divinity (Keller and Schneider, "Introduction," 1). A response to *Polydoxy*, like the practice of polydox theology itself, must then operate in variegated registers. A Christian theology that recognizes the differences among its own sources while remaining faithful in its commitments to, in Marcella Althaus-Reid's terms, the God whose back is made of difference,[2] will necessarily be an open-ended theology. After all, the most firmly established canon of Christian interpretation is that Christians do not agree on it. Christianity is *always* polydox, as the authors of *Polydoxy* remind us (Schneider, "Crib notes from Bethlehem," 21). As a theological method, polydoxy does not then transplant the practice of Christian theology into strange territory, despite its recommendation of "[a] responsible pluralism of interdependence and uncertainty" against Christian theology's apparent insistence on singularity in its approach to the uniqueness of its divinity (Keller and Schneider, "Introduction," 1). Valuing polydoxy rather than

Linn Marie Tonstad
Yale Divinity School, 409 Prospect Street, New Haven, CT 06511, USA
Email: linn.tonstad@yale.edu

[1] Catherine Keller and Laurel C. Schneider (eds), *Polydoxy: Theology of Multiplicity and Relation* (New York: Routledge, 2011), 1, emphasis in original. Subsequent references to *Polydoxy* will be cited internally according to author, title, and page number.
[2] Marcella Althaus-Reid, *The Queer God* (New York: Routledge, 2003), 16.

denying its existence permits theology to confess its pluriform nature openly rather than insisting on its own monofidelity.

Many feminist, womanist, and queer theologians have refused to submit fully to the disciplinary constraints of systematic theology, even as their projects are driven by visions of the God-world relation that are systematic in a slightly different sense. Highly legitimate concerns about phallogocentrism, Eurocentrism, and totalization combine with the influence of methods derived from social and cultural theory to render feminist, womanist, and queer theologians skeptical of the viability and desirability of systematic projects. Systematization implies the establishment of a structure of interpretation; if what is being interpreted is both in motion and structured by differentials of power, viability, and recognition, then attempts to develop such a structure may be false and implicated in injustice. Indeed, theology has in many cases not merely permitted but actively promoted the dehumanization of its racial, sexual, and religious "others". Whether expressed through Audre Lorde's agenda-setting challenge regarding the suitability of the master's tools for dismantling the master's house or in Althaus-Reid's invocation of women philosophers who live with broken hearts, many theologians have come to believe that the models and methods of classical systematic theology simply cannot be adapted to good use; at best, they may be redeployed mimetically, ironically, and absurdly for deconstructive and liberative purposes.[3]

To write theology as a queer and feminist theologian with a dogmatic orientation raises the question of whether these different discourses—queer theory, feminist theology and theory, and systematic theology—should be brought together despite the ambivalent and often antagonistic relations they have with one another. Is it possible to claim identifications (not identities) like "queer" and "feminist" and yet to come out as a lover of dogmatics? Or must dogmatic loves be sacrificed on the altar of the need to shift Christian discourses into non-dogmatic spaces for the sake of the future of queers, women, and the earth? The authors of *Polydoxy* answer the latter question with a qualified "no." Polydoxy comes to view inside, and at the unstable boundaries of, Christian contexts and commitments, and serves as a theological method of faithful engagement with multiple discourses. It provides a road map for the development and analysis of theological proposals that discover their friends in unexpected encounters.

Polydox theology's high valuation of uncertainty, openendedness, and relationality implies that its dogmatic proposals are offered in non-dogmatic

---

[3] See Audre Lorde, "The Master's Tools Will Never Dismantle the Master's House", in *Sister Outsider: Essays and Speeches* (Berkeley, ca: Crossing Press, 1984 [2007]), 110–113 and Althaus-Reid, *Queer God*, 48: "the obliteration of filiations, that sense of love towards the master's narrative which is so difficult to avoid and creates so many broken hearts amongst women philosophers."

fashion (see Faber, "The sense of peace: a para-doxology of divine multiplicity," 51). A non-dogmatic approach to dogmatics suggests that theological statements are offered in experimental mode. Exploring a dogmatic proposal concerning a particular theological topic or claim then requires testing it or experimenting with it to see what consequences it entails, whether in the mode of foreclosure or in the mode of possibility. Such experimentation might take the form of examining its implications for other dogmatic loci, as classical systematic theology habitually does. Theological proposals can also be tested for their plausibility, consistency, or viability from other directions. In practice, the outcomes of theological experiments result from complex negotiations between author, reader, argument, and genre. These results are discovered only in the performance of the experiment, and not all experiments yield conclusive results. Not even the discourses that claim for themselves the most generous apportionment of God's deposit of authoritative reason in humankind can determine *a priori* the possible results of employing different methods, taken perhaps from outside theology, to interrogate, fructify, enliven, or reshape theological proposals.

Given the antagonisms between systematic theology and queer theory, for instance, a theological experiment that makes use of such methodologies in a serious fashion may involve forms of interrogation, examination, and mimetic re-reading that may seem unregulated by disciplinary canons—even absurd. Yet the performance of such theological experiments engages affective registers not usually available to the dry conventions of systematic theology, making the familiar strange again and re-presenting the shocking nature of Christian doxological claims. As Laurel Schneider argues, laughter and parody are "profoundly serious" ways to shift the relations between "triumphal arches, solemn processions and avowals of holy innocence in the midst of genocidal advances and purges" (see Schneider, "Crib notes from Bethlehem," 21).[4] Even in the form of parody, absurdity can be a way to touch the holy aslant, in the very sites in which the holy (re)presents itself. Absurdity may also protect against the "desiccation" that follows theology's assumption of the success of its own definitional categories (Schneider, "Crib notes from Bethlehem," 28–9). Clinging to impropriety may serve as a form of reverence before a mystery that cannot be contained and locked down, no matter how hard we try (and try we do) to take refuge from wonder's terrifying and alluring depths in "hypercertainties" (Rivera, "Glory: the first passion of theology?" 174). But, as Catherine Keller writes, the "doctrinal protect[ion of] uncontrollability ... knows its own incapacity to know the infinite" (Keller, "Be a multiplicity: ancestral anticipations," 95–6). From this direction, one role impropriety plays in theological systems is as a reminder

---

[4] Schneider also emphasizes that theology's refusal of humor is accompanied by "over-reliance on apodictic and deductive modes of reasoning," 21.

of language's non-transparency to God. The always-riven linguistic materiality of theological reflection displays its wounds and incapacities as a form of
faithful piety.

In this article, I perform such an experiment on a particular claim in
contemporary trinitarian theology, that God the Father is *most truly* father in
such a way that divine fatherhood is neither a human projection nor tainted
by association with patriarchal or inadequate forms of human fatherhood. I
test the viability and plausibility of this claim using methods taken from
feminist and queer theory as well as from classical systematic theology,
moving from more recognizable genres of systematic theology into modes of
absurdity and mimesis taken from feminist and queer theological genres. The
examination of the logic of transcendence that theologians assert on behalf of
divine fatherhood opens up into a rereading of the trinitarian imaginary that
clarifies other ways in which the trinitarian persons come to be gendered.

This article thus makes three arguments in tightly interwoven fashion. The
first argument, expressed in the most general terms, is that an experimental
approach to theology that tests dogmatic claims using methods taken from
outside theology nonetheless may serve as a valuable test of the success of
theological assertions and of the means by which theological claims achieve
their ends. In this case, the primary claim being tested is an oft-repeated
assertion in contemporary trinitarian theology, even on occasion among
theologians who purport to maintain feminist commitments. The second
argument reflects the particular claim being tested. I show that the way four
theologians develop their cases for the truth and transcendence of divine
fatherhood preserves and indeed tightens the connection between divine and
human fatherhood—a connection which all four theologians seek to avoid.
This argument expands into a rereading of trinitarian structures of kinship, in
which I show that symbolic divine gendering is the result of multiple trinitarian grammars, not simply or even primarily the maleness of some of the
divine names.[5] The third argument is structural. This article uses different
genres to make two different kinds of arguments. While either type of argument *could* stand on its own, their interrelation strengthens—or so I propose—the power and the persuasiveness of each. If the reader is persuaded
that the arguments are stronger together, the implication of the structural
argument is that both classical systematic theology and feminist and queer
theology may become better—more persuasive, more alluring, more truth-
ful—if classical systematic theologians learn from feminist and queer theologians what realistic tests of their own proposals require, and if feminist and
queer theologians take the forms of assertion and argument on which classical systematic theology depends more seriously than is sometimes the case.
Doing the detailed work of engagement with classical theological discourses

---

[5] It is worth emphasizing that my argument here is neither that *all* father-language for God is
projection nor that God must *never* be named "Father."

while throwing up admittedly experimental theological proposals may do something to further a transformation of systematic theological discourse such that "feminist" theology would become indistinguishable from "Christian" theology—which, for a confessional feminist Christian theologian like myself, is an orientation of desire. The practice of polyfidelity to these divergent discourses means that these allegedly "particularist" theologies can no longer be relegated to the margins of Christian theology as supplementary additions to an already set field of discourse.[6] Instead, feminist, womanist, and queer visions can and must reshape what counts as the field of systematic theological practice.

Experimental theology

In a polydox Christian theology that values multiplicity, the God of whom theology speaks takes trinitarian form. It is telling that three of the thirteen essays in *Polydoxy*—Keller's, Thatamanil's, and Lee's—focus in some way on the—or a—trinity, and particularly on the positive potential of the Spirit. The argument below will support this sense of the Spirit's potential. But the trinity does not lend itself easily to the ends that many contemporary theological projects seek. Such ends are well expressed by John Thatamanil: "One conviction that drives the resurgence of trinitarianism is the notion that trinity offers a promising resource for social ontology. If to be is to be in relation, then there is no clearer paradigm for that contention than the trinity itself" (Thatamanil, "God as ground, contingency, and relation: trinitarian polydoxy and religious diversity," 239). While Thatamanil rightly identifies the reason for much recent interest in the trinity, I am unconvinced by the second assertion, and in general about the usefulness of trinitarianism for the development of a social ontology. If to be is to be in relation, which is irreducibly true of all human experience material and social—and there is no immaterial and asocial human experience—then we do not need the trinity to discover the priority of relation. What we purport to learn of relation from the trinity is better learned elsewhere.[7] For us, the question of what *sorts of* relations we are in becomes much more pressing than the bare assertion of relationality itself.

The authors of the essays in *Polydoxy* already know that the fundamental question is the shape of relation rather than its facticity (see, for example, Betcher, "Take my yoga upon you: a spiritual pli for the global city," 68–70).

---

[6] I borrow the term "polyfidelity" as a name for the theological method of polydoxy from Althaus-Reid, who distinguishes polyfidelity from "a familiar biblical contractual model [in which] the relationship with the 'Jealous God' of Israel is linked to particular forms of understanding property and the body as property"; *Queer God*, 128–129.

[7] In recent theology, this argument has been made most forcefully by Kathryn Tanner. See especially chapter 5, "Politics", in *Christ the Key* (Cambridge: Cambridge University Press, 2010) 207–46.

But the case for trinitarian relationality as a promising site for theological reflection has been made in myriad other registers as well. Indeed, systematic theologians have generated bookcases full of text on the trinity's promise in recent decades. That promise has primarily been oriented toward the bettering of social relations, but it has by no means been limited to that realm. Truth, revelation, theological epistemology, liturgical fidelity, self-sacrifice, obedience, the undoing of sexism, God's identification with the suffering victim, and the presence of the future in history are all themes that have been grounded in trinitarian dogmatics in such works. The revealed knowledge of the triune God has promised the undoing of sedimented logics in Christianity's intertwining with injustice, ontological hierarchies, and the love of the one over the love of the other. But diagnosing the ways in which trinitarian theology continues to serve hierarchies of gender and sexuality is a task not yet completed in the canons of systematic theology. Such diagnostic engagement may provide support for the constructive re-readings of Christian and other traditions that dominate the *Polydoxy* volume.

Multiplicity, open-endedness, and uncertainty are values that serve to hold open dogmatic claims in anti-idolatrous fashion. Incongruity, experimentation, and mimesis are all forms of idolatry-critique within Christian thought. Mimetic incongruity (doing theology askew, with respect to both method and predication) is a constantly moving resource for indicating theology's failures and the absurdity of its own attempts to speak God; it also grounds theology in biblical traditions of language use (God as rock, for instance) and in the confounding of the wise (1. Cor. 1:27). Indeed, twisting language beyond its everyday usage is intrinsic to theology's practice in its most classical forms. Concepts are taken from non-theological discourses and "skewed" for the theological purposes for which they are adopted,[8] while retaining some of the initial registers of meaning that render the terms appropriate to their theological adaptations.[9] Language has been purged sufficiently for theological use only after undergoing such redefinition. This kind of speech, in its juxtaposition of incongruous images for God, serves as a kataphatic practice of theological apophaticism: the proliferation of speech in service of speech's failure to capture its referent.[10] Even so, such language still has to be tested in its concrete deployment to see whether the relation

---

[8] Thomas Aquinas argues that while some terms may be predicated of God substantially, their mode of signification still derives from creatures. *How* the terms mean is distinguished from *what* the terms mean. See Aquinas, *Summa Theologica*, part I, QQ. 1–26, Fathers of the English Dominican Province (trans), second edition (London: Burns Oates & Washbourne, 1912), Ia, Q. 13.2, Q.13.3 and Q. 13.6 (where Aquinas's sed contra is Eph. 3:14–15, to which we return below), 152–56 and 162–64.

[9] See Kathryn Tanner, *God and Creation in Christian Theology: Tyranny or Empowerment?* (Minneapolis, MN: Fortress Press, 2005 [reprint]), 26–7 and 54–5.

[10] Here I follow Denys Turner, as in for instance "Apophaticism, Idolatry and the Claims of Reason", in Oliver Davies and Denys Turner (eds), *Silence and the Word: Negative Theology and Incarnation* (Cambridge: Cambridge University Press, 2002), 16–18.

between a term's ordinary uses and its theological valences is sufficiently askew to prevent the accidental importation of the very aspects of the term's definition its theological twisting is intended to rule out.

Any test of the relation between theology's uses of a term and its ordinary meanings must then also take place inside a theological imaginary on the level of its *Wirkungsmittel* (the means by which it enacts its effects)—not just through its philosophical and theological definitions and distinctions, but also according to the images that enliven it. The metaphorical and imagistic registers of a theological project regularly overtake its stipulative limitations. When theologians insist that Jesus' physical masculinity grounds a symbolic system in which only males may act *in persona christi*, while the theological significance of femininity is limited to creation's consensual acceptance of a divine initiative, for instance, no insistence that "these symbol systems do not imply gender hierarchy or inequality" can trump their establishment in fact. Such factical hierarchies need to be identified and combated through the development of alternative proposals that point out the theological failures on which these hierarchies depend. But imagistic registers often function with greater effectiveness precisely because their power is not utterly subjected to the discipline of definition in the theological task. Interpretations of the symbolic system of a theological imaginary need not then limit themselves exclusively to the denotative register. Since those images and rhetorical strategies illustrate, vivify, and make plausible theology's stipulations, they must be read also on their own terms, especially to see where and how they transgress the limitations imposed by the definitional usages to which they are responsible.

Yet such transgression of the stipulative limitations of theology also requires serious engagement with the ways in which theologians defend themselves against the apparent implications of the proposals they advance. Taking the technical distinctions of classical theology seriously does not mean uncritical acceptance of the existing, always contested, discursive structures of the field, but it does require showing precisely how, where, and why those distinctions fail or require revision. Doing the detailed work of engagement is only in part a tactical move made necessary by the disciplinary conservatism of theology. The systematicity of theology is a site of positive power as much as of failure, and its value can neither be denied nor overwritten by fiat. Absurdity and impropriety might thus serve as productive ways to determine where technical distinctions fail, or require redefinition. Yet staying on the level of the absurd is not enough by itself. Absurd misreadings of theological technicalities might subsequently undergo a second translation back into the sober idiom and genre of theology, generating new skew(er)ings, new stipulations, and different relations among the very technicalities just subjected to the test. These reordered technicalities may also be brought to bear inside constructive theological systems on their own, without their strange histories being visible at first glance. Thus the heavy burden of orthodoxy's sedimentation, lightened by the lever provided by the slanting language of absurdity, sits less revengefully on the theologian's bowed shoulders.

So much for how this article makes its argument and why it makes it in such fashion. Let us turn to the experiment, which moves from the genre of classical systematic theology into increasingly absurd and incongruous mimetic registers in the development of its argument. The conclusion then returns to the sober genre more typical of systematic theology to suggest some implications of the experiment for constructive trinitarian theology.

The transcendent Father and his others

If the phallus *must* negate the penis in order to symbolize and signify in its privileged way, then the phallus is bound to the penis, not through simple identity, but through determinate negation. If the phallus only signifies to the extent that it is *not* the penis, and the penis is qualified as that body part that it must *not be*, then the phallus is fundamentally dependent upon the penis in order to symbolize at all. Indeed, the phallus would be nothing without the penis. And in that sense in which the phallus requires the penis for its own constitution, the identity of the phallus includes the penis, that is, a relation of identity holds between them. And this is, of course, not only a logical point, for we have seen that the phallus not only opposes the penis in a logical sense, but is itself instituted through the repudiation of its partial, decentered, and substitutable character.[11]

Christian theologians say that to address God as "Father" is not to claim that God is a father *like* any other; to say that God is Father is to say that God is a father *unlike* any other. God's fatherhood entails neither maleness nor biological reproduction, for instance. Divine paternity means that God the Father alone begets a Son who is all that the Father is (the perfect image of the Father), without interval (there is no separation between them), without confusion (the Son never becomes a father, and the Father is not the Son), and without multiplication (the persons of the trinity are one non-numerically-multipliable God). These statements refract language into new registers of meaning in which the term "father" goes awry from its ordinary usage. Indeed, the meaning of the term "Father" for God is non-luminous to those who use it, since only the Father and the Son know what it means to say that one begets the other.[12] In order to avoid the dangers of idolatry and projection, trinitarian theologians commonly emphasize that God is Father neither in a literal nor in a generic sense, but only in relation to the Son. But learning that "Father" in

---

[11] Judith Butler, *Bodies that Matter* (New York: Routledge, 1993), 84.

[12] Gregory of Nazianzus, "The Theological Orations," in Edward R. Hardy (ed), *Christology of the Later Fathers* (Louisville, KY: Westminster John Knox, 2006 [1954]), 164–165.

God means only "the Father of the Son" still implies that using father rightly means remembering that God is not *a* father, but a father of a different sort than any and all others.[13] So although the believer may not know just what it means to call God father, the believer must learn what it does *not* mean to call God father—as Nazianzen says, "The Father is the begetter and the emitter; *without* passion, of course, and *without* reference to time, and *not* in a corporeal manner."[14] The fundamental relation between divine and human fatherhood is thus one of dissimilarity. Yet a very common strategy that theologians employ as a marker of that dissimilarity turns out to generate similarity, and indeed a form of identity, where none such ought to be.

Appeals to the transcendent and analogy-bursting character of God's fatherhood have become an increasingly common defensive strategy among theologians who wish feminist criticism to touch only the edges of the deposit of faith. As Hans Urs von Balthasar phrases it, Jesus "calls [him] 'Father' in a sense that bursts all analogies."[15] Or in William Placher's terms, "What it means that Jesus has a divine Father, and that we are allowed to call this one our 'Father,' transcends every human case of fatherhood."[16] Thomas Torrance likewise insists that

> the concepts of fatherhood and sonship do not derive from any analogy or inherent likeness between the creature and the Creator. They are laid hold of by divine revelation and are made to point back away altogether from their creaturely and human use to their creative source in the transcendent nature of God, who is eternally Father in himself. . . . Since man is created after the image of God, all fatherly relations within humanity derive from and point to the unique, aboriginal, and transcendent Fatherhood of God. Accordingly, human fatherhood may not be used as a standard by which to judge divine Fatherhood, for there is strictly no comparison between human fatherhood and divine Fatherhood. . . . On the contrary, it is according to the uncreated Fatherhood of God that all creaturely fatherhood is to be understood.[17]

---

[13] Even to set the comparison up in this way implies just what the comparison intends to deny—and what my argument in the rest of this article will challenge—namely that the relevant point of comparison for divine fatherhood is "other" fathers.

[14] Nazianzus, "Theological Orations," 161, emphasis added.

[15] Hans Urs von Balthasar, *Theo-Drama: Theological Dramatic Theory*, volume III, *The Dramatis Personae: The Person in Christ*, Graham Harrison (trans) (San Francisco, CA: Ignatius Press, 1992), 518. Balthasar connects the analogy-bursting character of divine fatherhood to the Father's generous begetting of the Son out of his womb. Balthasar, like Jürgen Moltmann, is a good example of how those who are considered only marginally orthodox are often the best routes into a diagnostic mapping of an imaginary, for marginal orthodoxy indicates a repetition with a terrifying difference—surfacing what orthodoxy most fears is the truth about its own narratives.

[16] William Placher, *The Triune God: An Essay in Postliberal Theology* (Louisville, KY: Westminster John Knox Press, 2007), 80.

[17] Thomas F. Torrance, "The Christian Apprehension of God the Father," in Alvin F. Kimel, Jr. (ed), *Speaking the Christian God: The Holy Trinity and the Challenge of Feminism* (Grand Rapids, MI:

Torrance's argument twists agonizingly as he insists that no comparison can be made between human and divine fatherhood, except that the former derives from the latter and so ought to be judged by it. He stretches to protect the downward derivation of paternity without introducing a corresponding upward signification: although there is nothing about creaturely fatherhood in general that makes it an appropriate revelatory vessel for the divine, the concept of fatherhood may by the grace of God become an image of the divine. But this statement is juxtaposed with the claim that there is no "analogy or inherent likeness" grounding the relation between divine and human fathers although the latter image the former and point to it as their ground, origin, and transcendent goal. The concepts of fatherhood and sonship cannot meaningfully point "away altogether" from the creaturely usages to which they are adapted by their divine origin, especially as *concepts*. Torrance continues, "we must think of the Fatherhood of God and the relation of human fatherhood to it in an altogether *spiritual* and *imageless* way, and thus without ever reading back descriptively into God the creaturely content or finite imagery of human fatherhood."[18] It is difficult to think of the fatherhood of God in an imageless way if all creaturely fatherhood is its image. But Torrance's primary fear is that human fatherhood might "judge" the divine kind or be projected into it; he seems to take for granted that human fatherhood actively images the divine. Perhaps Torrance's difficulties follow from the two irreconcilable New Testament texts he juxtaposes, Matt. 23:9 and Eph. 3:15.[19] The first enjoins the reservation of the title "father" only to God, while the second extends the name "Father" downward from God onto "every fatherhood in heaven and on earth." Torrance interprets this to mean that only God is properly father, while all other fathers are so only in a derivative sense. Yet if the divine signification of fatherhood brought with it other fathers or their attributes, it would be idolatrous rather than proper, as Torrance's rejection of analogy or likeness implies.[20] The signification of divine fatherhood thus depends on a successful distinction between it and the human kind.

William B. Eerdmans Publishing Company, 1992), 129–130. Torrance uses a passage from Karl Barth to support this point: "we do not call God Father because we know what that is; on the contrary, because we know God's Fatherhood we afterwards understand what human fatherhood truly is"; Karl Barth, *The Faith of the Church: A Commentary on the Apostles' Creed according to Calvin's Catechism*, Gabriel Vahanian (trans) (New York: Meridian Books, 1958), 14, quoted in Torrance, "Christian Apprehension," 130. See also 137, where Torrance again insists that "God alone is truly and ultimately Father—all other fatherhood is a reflection of his."

[18] Torrance, "Christian Apprehension," 130, emphasis in original. See also Thomas F. Torrance, *The Trinitarian Faith: The Evangelical Theology of the Ancient Catholic Church* (Edinburgh: T&T Clark, 1993), 70–72.

[19] Torrance, "Christian Apprehension," 131.

[20] Robert Jenson comments that "ideological opposition to use of 'Father' and 'Son' and so to the triune name has even led to the manifestly bogus claim that the triune name cannot be a 'proper' name just *because* it has descriptive meaning and so can be translated"; *Systematic Theology* vol. 1: *The Triune God* (Oxford: Oxford University Press, 1997), 45, footnote 28. Jenson

In another influential example of this strategy, Jürgen Moltmann distinguishes between patriarchal (or "monotheistic") and trinitarian concepts of fatherhood in God. The first type, "God the Father—the father of the church—the father of his country—the father of the family," establishes a chain of fathers who stand in analogous relationships to each other. Each father gains power from and in relation to the others, while supporting the others in turn. The second, trinitarian type focuses on the loving relationship between God the Father and God the Son, so that the Father's "fatherhood is defined by the relationship to this Son." A rather arduous process of training is required to disconnect one from the other, however: "anyone who wants to understand the trinitarian God must forget the ideas behind this patriarchal Father religion—the super-ego, the father of the family, the father of his country, even the 'fatherly providence'. He must gaze solely at the life and message of his brother Jesus: for in fellowship with the only begotten Son he will recognize that the Father of Jesus Christ is his Father too."[21] The Father who is discovered in that gaze is "a father who both begets and bears his son" and so becomes "a motherly father too."[22] Moltmann claims that "the doctrine of the Trinity" in this moment "makes a first approach towards overcoming sexist language in the concept of God."[23] Allowing God the Father, who is properly father in the trinity and adoptively father in relation to all other human beings, to transcend his patriarchal limitations by including even maternity within his all-encompassing grasp neither destabilizes divine patriarchy nor serves as an overcoming of sexism. After all, divine males get to be father, son, and mother, thus demonstrating that symbolic divine masculinity includes even maternity in its transcendent perfection. Non-divine females get to be—at best—included in the indeterminate and androgynous spirit and as symbolic adjuncts to the Father's ecstatic maternal self-realization. Ultimately, then, Moltmann's training cannot succeed, for it requires a constant reminder—a bind on the self—that *this* use of fatherhood is different from all other forms of the same. This disconnection establishes an irreducible relation between the different kinds of fatherhood as the self directs its attention to one of the forms and reminds itself that *that* one has nothing to do with *this* one. The self must continually submit itself to examination to ensure that it is looking only toward the right forms of fatherhood and disavowing the wrong ones. Such a repudiation effectively generates its own

---

is correct to identify such a claim as mistaken. The issue is not whether "Father" has descriptive meaning in addition to being a proper name (or "a term of address within a narrative construction that displays a relation internal to the logic of the construction," in Jenson's words). The challenge is whether and how such descriptive meanings are read into the name in ways that either result in the projection of creaturely characteristics into God or that tie God the Father to creaturely fathers in other ways.

[21] Jürgen Moltmann, *The Trinity and the Kingdom: The Doctrine of God*, Margaret Kohl (trans) (Minneapolis, MN: Fortress Press, 1993 [1981]), 163.

[22] Ibid., 164.

[23] Ibid., 165.

transgression by cementing a constitutive relation between these purport-edly different paternal deployments: remember to forget the patriarchal father, as it were! The result is precisely the opposite of what Moltmann says he intends. Other linguistic usages are able to distinguish the different mean-ings of the "same" term without just such arduous labor because the mean-ings and contextual deployments of the terms are transparently differentiable without the question of a positive relation (and thus the need to generate a distinction) between them arising in the first place. But in this case, the activity of the believer in gazing *only* in the right (and not the wrong) direction suggests just how closely divine fatherhood and human patriarchy are tied together. Indeed, the specific term "father" has shown itself as a potent inflammation to Christian practices of gendered hierarchies, espe-cially in combination with the theological significance often given to the maleness of Christ and his disciples. So the disconnection Moltmann requires is from Christianity's own history, and that history is the trinity's history too.

Wolfhart Pannenberg admits that the use of "father"-language for God derives from patriarchal social organization.[24] Yet "[t]o bring sexual differen-tiation into the understanding of God would mean polytheism," so the God of Israel has "no female partner" (although Pannenberg neglects the signifi-cance of Israel's symbolic femininity to this point).[25] Interestingly, Pannenberg reads the *social* role of the father as more theologically decisive than its gendered or biological aspects. Christ's revelation of God the Father transforms the meaning of divine fatherhood into something like "the duty of a family head to care for the members." Of course, the father is no longer the "head of the family" in many contexts, which might seem to invalidate the analogy. But for Pannenberg, such shifting relations do "not justify the demand for a revision of the concept of God as Father" because such revision would imply that theology is no more than projection. Instead, Pannenberg identifies election and covenant as the substantial and material forms that divine fatherhood takes.

> These features can then be taken up into an understanding of God which confronts the changing concept of human fatherhood as a *norm*. In com-parison with it all human fatherhood also pales. For this reason it still retains its power even at a time when patriarchal forms decay and the role of the father within the family loses its distinctive contours. Then the fatherhood of God can truly become the epitome of God's comprehen-sive care—the type of care which human fatherhood can *no longer* offer.[26]

---

[24] Wolfhart Pannenberg, *Systematic Theology*, vol. 1, Geoffrey W. Bromiley (trans) (Grand Rapids, MI: William B. Eerdmans Publishing Company, 1991), 260.

[25] Ibid., 261. As Pannenberg says, "A mark of Israel's faith from the very outset is that the God who elected the patriarchs, the God of the exodus and Sinai, has no female partner."

[26] Ibid., 262, latter emphasis mine. Walter Kasper makes an almost identical claim: "the covenantal idea of God as Father can be turned in a prophetic and critical way against the

Divine paternal care confronts failing human paternity (partial, decentered, and substitutable as the latter is) with its own comprehensiveness, its own exemplary nature, and its own unsubstitutability. Pannenberg, tellingly, construes this as a defense against, rather than a validation of, feminist criticisms of the patriarchal nature of the father-god. He continues,

> For all his subjection to the Father, Jesus undoubtedly claimed that God is to be understood only as the heavenly Father whom he declared him to be. . . . Jesus is the Son inasmuch as it is in his message of the nearness of the royal rule of the Father, his subjection to the Father's will, and especially the function of his sending as a revelation of the love of God, that this God may be known as Father.[27]

Amazingly, the *subjection* of the Son to the Father reveals the non-patriarchal nature of divine fatherhood. For Pannenberg, the Son's citational practice (obedient submission via invocation or repetition of the law of the Father as the only God) activates and secures his divinity. Jesus' constant insistence that his Other is the lawgiver to whom he submits enacts the truth of the Father's delegation of his authority to the Son.[28] *This* is the mode of Jesus' sonship, revealing the deeper reason, beyond extrapolation from the assumption of Jesus' maleness, why he is *son* in the theological imaginary. As the one who becomes the eternal locus of the Father's monarchy in this submission, the Son's subjection is a form of kenotic participation in the power of paternity, the form of fatherhood that remains bound to its human instantiation through determinate negation.

In her influential essay, "Can a Feminist Call God 'Father'?" Janet Martin Soskice picks up Moltmann's attempt to identify the Father only through the Son's revelation of him, rather than via any general concept of fatherhood.[29] But in the lightly revised version of the essay that appears in her recent book

---

concrete fathers of this world. In all truth the dignity of father belongs to God alone. It is not any earthly father but God, from whom all fatherhood is derived (Eph. 3.15), who defines what true fatherhood is. . . . God's fatherhood, being the source, is also the norm of paternal authority and the critical standard by which it is judged"; Matthew J. O'Connell (trans), *The God of Jesus Christ* (New York: Crossroad, 1997), 139–140. Kasper claims that sexism is excluded nonetheless since "the Old Testament can also translate the Father's loving mercy into the language of womanliness and motherhood," 140.

[27] Pannenberg, *Systematic Theology*, vol. 1, 264.

[28] Pannenberg argues that it belongs to the concept of God that God must be lord of any actually existing world. The materialization and establishment of God's lordship in the world is the task of the Son and Spirit; this extension outward of the inner-trinitarian monarchy is the link between economic and immanent trinity. For a more extensive discussion of these issues, see my " 'The ultimate consequence of his self-distinction from the Father . . .': Difference and Hierarchy in Pannenberg's Trinity", *Neue Zeitschrift für Systematische Theologie und Religionsphilosophie* 51 (2009), 383–399.

[29] Janet Martin Soskice, "Can a Feminist Call God 'Father'?" in Teresa Elwes (ed), *Women's Voices: Essays in Contemporary Feminist Theology* (London: Marshall Pickering, 1992), 15–29. Also printed in Kimel, *Speaking the Christian God*, 81–94.

The Kindness of God, Soskice, in an astonishingly revealing move, begins her discussion with the human rather than divine version of the same:

> Fathers, of any sort, get only bad press these days. Fathers—as fathers—seem only to appear in the press if associated with criminal violence of a sexual, physical, or psychological sort (usually all three) towards partners, wives, or children. Or else they appear as absent. Single parent families are overwhelmingly headed by women, while "fathers" cannot, or will not, be found. Yet in the biblical writings, naming God "Father" is an anticipation of great intimacy, new relation, of hope, and of love.[30]

Although her discussion aims to distinguish and even separate divine paternity from the human kind, it starts *from* human paternity. And not just from human paternity in general, but from the "absence" of fathers in single-parent families, and from the "bad press" that *all* fathers get these days. The evidence for such bad press is lacking—Soskice simply leaves the assertion hanging. Her contrast between the desirability and uniqueness of theo-biblical paternity with the failures—real and representational—of human paternity serves to cement an already-existing relation between them rather than disconnecting one from the other. Soskice is concerned, however, to block the undesirable consequences of an unchastened divine paternity: "what is objectionable is . . . that the 'divine male' is styled as one who is powerful, dominant, and implacable."[31] Here Soskice mistakenly identifies the almighty and overbearing aspects of divine paternity as the problem with it. She assumes that a gentle, kind, and consent-seeking divine father would be less susceptible to idolatry, and less susceptible to deployment in the establishment of gendered human hierarchies, but there is no reason to believe that, nor is any argument offered. Indeed, the trope of the benevolent patriarch or head of the family lies at least as deep in our cultural registers as does that of the "implacable" male, as Pannenberg's discussion shows.[32] Soskice develops her benevolent father in relation to another programmatic essay, Paul Ricoeur's "Fatherhood: From Phantasm to Symbol,"[33] in which he argues that representations of fatherhood develop and change

---

[30] Janet Martin Soskice, *The Kindness of God: Metaphor, Gender, and Religious Language* (Oxford: Oxford University Press, 2008), 66.

[31] Ibid., 71.

[32] Soskice assumes that there is such a thing as *"the* feminist objection" (ibid., 72, emphasis added) to father-language for God, which may be why she holds that the particular form of divine masculinity is the problem. She connects the objection to Sallie McFague's rejection of omnipotence and otherness in descriptions of God. But there is no intrinsic connection between being concerned about father-language for God and rejecting divine omnipotence. It is perfectly possible to hold on to classical understandings of divine omnipotence yet to have concerns about the function of father-language for God.

[33] Paul Ricoeur, "Fatherhood: From Phantasm to Symbol," in Don Ihde (ed), *The Conflict of Interpretations: Essays in Hermeneutics* (Evanston, IL: Northwestern University Press, 1974), 468–497.

in the biblical materials, moving toward an ever-greater intimacy grounded in the Son's knowledge of the Father. As Soskice summarizes part of his argument, "The God of Israel is defined, then, over and against father gods, gods who beget the world, and paradoxically, it is this abolition of the bio-logical father God that makes non-idolatrous, metaphorical 'father language' about God possible."[34] Human fatherhood is qualified as the thing that divine fatherhood *must not* be. When Soskice claims that an "incomplete [Father-]figure … traverses a number of semantic levels"[35] in order to escape its patriarchal determination, she returns to the arguments devel-oped by Moltmann above regarding the motherly Father and the priority of the Son's revelation of the Father.[36] And so we have come full circle.

These wonderfully non-patriarchal father-figments of the theological imagination slide back and forth between divine and human fatherhood. Their relations to each other can be measured in units derived from the slippage between the phallus and the penis. One is established by a specific repudiation of the other, ensuring that they are not only bound together, but the divine achieves what the human should have been, but never can be. The asserted transcendence of human fatherhood is vitiated in that move. Divine paternity is not like human paternity—it is not fragmented and vulnerable to failure, nor is it in need of intercourse (and therefore an unreliable erection) or a sexually differentiated other. What divine paternity is *not* like is human paternity specifically, not, say, human relations of care more generally. Yet in these theologies, divine paternity is the origin of all paternity and all relationality in its generation of the Son, and its perfection further serves to critique the failure of human paternity, the all-embracing care that cannot be offered by a merely human father. So human paternity remains a reflection of

---

[34] Soskice, *Kindness*, 76.

[35] Soskice does not insist that God ought *only* to be addressed as Father. She follows Susan Brooks Thistlethwaite in admitting that divine father-language may carry dangerous associations for women who have been abused by their fathers (Soskice, *Kindness*, 81–82). I would suggest, however, that divine father-language is not merely risky due to the abusive behavior of some human fathers, but because when used in the ways examined here, it establishes fatherhood as a particular reflection of God and, conversely, God as a particularly excellent kind of father by which other fathers should be measured.

[36] When Soskice tells her trinitarian story briefly in the following chapter (Soskice, *Kindness*, 116), she argues, following Jean-Luc Marion, that God the Father "in some sense" also dies on the cross with the Son, then " 'is born'—or better 'becomes father'—with the Son and in the Spirit. This is a vision of a Trinity of complete mutuality" (ibid., 117). It is difficult to sort out the metaphysics of such a claim, especially since Soskice retains a classical account of the processions without quite explaining the different levels of predication with which she operates. An economy in which the Father too dies, and which reads the cross as the "*separation* of God from God" (emphasis added) offers little promise for life and hope and obscures the copresence of the trinitarian persons with each other in the economy of salvation. Immanently, she suggests, this "is a story of the perichoretic outpouring of love and birth between the three who *are* only in relation one to another. All three persons, figuratively, give birth"—the Father to the Son, the Son to the church, and the Spirit who "animates the Church in the world" (ibid., 119). Yet it is only the Father who begets the Son, while the Spirit gives birth only to that which is non-divine.

its divine archetype and participates in its imagistic power. The use to which these theologians put divine fatherhood establishes, rather than negates, a positive relation between divine and human fatherhood. And this happens just at the point at which that relation is denied. Indeed, this identification is the result of the specific strategies used as defensive measures *against* the suspicion that God the Father may have anything to do with fatherhood more generally.

But let us examine the structure of the trinitarian imaginary yet more carefully. The discussion hitherto has focused on the specific quilting point of the relation between divine and human fatherhood. If these theologians insist, as indeed they do, that it is only in relation to the Son that the Father is known as Father, and that the fatherhood revealed in that relation looks quite different than any other kind of fatherhood (although the latter might nonetheless be the point of comparison and distinction for the former), then we must test such claims as well. The imaginary expressed in the trinitarian register must, these theologians suggest, retain no patriarchal forms of fatherhood derived from the cultural imaginary of masculinity. That would be to look at other fathers only to project their attributes into God. Perhaps innertrinitarian fatherhood might yet surprise us with its difference—whether in practice or in representation—from ordinary human fatherhood. Perhaps *this* examination will at last show us the Father-God who is neither male nor patriarchal as we approach him from his relation to the Son and Spirit.

Arguably, the most significant difference between "Eastern" and "Western" trinitarianisms is the issue of the *filioque* clause, which in the West stabilizes the distinction between the Son and Spirit by introducing an oppositional relation between them. In the East, the distinction is guaranteed by *the name*, the law of the Father, who *begets* one and *brings forth* the other. The distinction between the Son and the Spirit is found not in their relation one to the other, which is subsequent in a non-temporal sense to their originary relations to the Father, but in the monarchical act of "production" or causation.[37] It is not irrelevant that the East accepts the terminology of "cause" that the West rejects. The former accepts the subordinationist consequences of this picture, indeed celebrates them, as a manifestation of the all-encompassing monarchy of the Father, whose person alone is self-grounding freedom in ecstatic mode.[38] The latter, worried about subordination and ontological distinction, subjects the Father also *to* the law of trinitarian differentiation by the

---

[37] See Vladimir Lossky, *In The Image and Likeness of God* (Crestwood, NY: St. Vladimir's Seminary Press, 1974), 82; John Zizioulas, *Being as Communion: Studies in Personhood and the Church* (Crestwood, NY: St. Vladimir's Seminary Press, 1997), 40; Gregory of Nyssa, "An Answer to Ablabius: That We Should Not Think of Saying There Are Three Gods," in *Christology of the Later Fathers*, 266–267; contrast Thomas Aquinas, *Summa Theologica* part I, QQ. 27–49, Fathers of the English Dominican Province (trans), second edition (London: Burns Oates & Washbourne, 1921), Ia, Q. 27.1, pp. 3–6 and especially Q. 33.1, pp. 72–73.
[38] Zizioulas, *Being as Communion*, 44–46, esp. footnote 40.

addition of the words "and [through] the Son" to secure the difference of the Spirit from the Son. In the West, then, the monarchy of the Father is insufficient by itself to guarantee the distinction between the Son and Spirit. Monarchy and productive power are finally non-identical and to an extent transferable (heritable), for only the productive power of the Father, not his monarchy, is transferred to the Son as the latter participates in breathing out the Spirit, and only the Son receives the name of the Father. This law of the Son sets him up as a second origin within the trinity. He becomes another "father" whose fatherhood is simultaneously secured and cancelled out through the name "Son," which derives from and extends the name "Father." Reproduction of the name in derived mode, or what we might term the trinitarian structure of kinship, functions to safeguard relation and inheritance. The Spirit is the hidden location of these exchanges of inheritance, monarchy, and the name. Thus the femininity of the Spirit has proven itself the irresistible condition of trinitarian exogamy as the second difference or as the bond of the mutual love of Father and Son.[39] The Spirit's escape from paternal over-determination is also its subjection and its forgetting.

The trinitarian system of differentiation and distinction works through the appearance of the Father's generative power, which expresses itself in the Word of difference: the Son, who is the perfect image of the Father and the guarantor of his fecundity. The Son is the Word according to whom all of reality is structured and brought into being as an ordered unity; the Son is also the Father's phallus as the symbol and sign of the Father's plenitude. The phallus, symbolically speaking, is the sign of meaning's stabilization and so of the possibility of plenitudinous self-identity.[40] The Father is only himself in the generation of the Son,[41] so the generation of the Son stabilizes and secures the Father's ecstatic self-identity as Father. Moreover, the perfection of the Son's imaging of the Father means that the difference of the Son is only a difference of origin, yet a difference that shows itself as obedience and gratitude.[42] The Son is also the Father's seed, not just as the *logos spermatikos*

---

[39] Several patristic references to the feminine Spirit can be found in Joel C. Elowsky (ed), *We Believe in the Holy Spirit*, in *Ancient Christian Doctrine 4* (Downers Grove, IL: IVP Academic, 2009), 18. Leonardo Boff refers approvingly to the "feminine dimension" of the Spirit in Phillip Berryman (trans), *Holy Trinity, Perfect Community* (Maryknoll, NY: Orbis Books, 2000), 92–93, although he adds the usual caveats about God being beyond gender. The appeal to the Spirit's femininity is common enough that Mary Daly's mimicking of such appeals has not yet been surpassed: "You're included under the Holy Spirit. He's feminine!"; *Gyn/Ecology: The Metaethics of Radical Feminism* (Boston, MA: Beacon Press, 1990 [1978]), 38.

[40] In the trinity, sign and signified coincide in the relation between the Father and his Word.

[41] "For without the Son the Father has neither existence nor name, any more than the Powerful without Power, or the Wise without Wisdom." Gregory of Nyssa, *Against Eunomius*, in Philip Schaff and Rev. Henry Wallace (eds), *Nicene and Post-Nicene Fathers*, vol. V, Second Series (New York: Cosimo Classics, 2007), book II, section 3, 105.

[42] "In fact, the Son's absolute obedience 'even unto death, the death of the Cross' is intrinsically oriented to the Father (otherwise it would be meaningless, and not in any case an absolute

but also as the seed that in its death fructifies the womb of Mary-church.[43] The Father's power of self-sharing shows his humility (in his willingness to share himself with another) and just so his supreme, absolute power (for a father who can share himself and all his power fully with another, without being threatened by that other, is greater than a father who cannot[44]). And the fullness of trinitarian distinctiveness shows itself as Father and Son breathe out an Other who is the sign and seal of the perfection—the virginal purity—of their mutual love.[45]

The Holy Spirit serves as the site for the preservation of the self-identity of Father and Son by protecting their focus on each other while purportedly freeing them from the charge of narcissism or self-enclosure (trinitarian theologians like to emphasize that love must always have a third[46]). The Spirit's ambiguous escape has a positive and a negative aspect: positively, as the name which points to the divine being (for God is spirit),[47] and negatively, as the specular other of Father and Son in which they gaze at one another, an infinite mirroring traceable back to the Father's self-imaging in his Other. If the Holy Spirit secures the relation between Father and Son, the Spirit's disappearance, its absence from the scene of figuration, is made evident. Or perhaps the Spirit is the sign and seal of the fecundity of the Father-Son relationship. Then the Father's paternal virility is secured through the generation of the Son, which leaves his womb empty[48] because his *all* (except fatherhood) is given in the begetting (not making) of this Son. The Father's womb renders him auto-erotically penetrable without fragmenting him, for his "emptiness" is only symbolic as his Word speaks of love in the breathing out of the Spirit, showing that he comes over and over again in an endless and

---

divine obedience)"; Hans Urs von Balthasar, *Mysterium Paschale: The Mystery of Easter*, Aidan Nichols, OP (trans) (San Francisco, CA: Ignatius Press, 1990), 208.

[43] Hans Urs von Balthasar, *Theo-drama: Theological Dramatic Theory*, volume IV: *The Action*, Graham Harrison (trans) (San Francisco, CA: Ignatius Press, 1994), 351–361, especially 361: "the Word is empowered to make his whole body into God's seed; thus the Word finally and definitively becomes flesh in the Virgin Mother, Mary-Ecclesia."

[44] See, for instance, Richard of St. Victor, *The Trinity*, in Grover A. Zinn (trans) *Richard of St Victor: The Twelve Patriarchs, The Mystical Ark, Book Three of the Trinity* (New York: Paulist Press, 1979), book 3, chapter IV, 376–77.

[45] As, again, Richard of St. Victor suggests (ibid., book 3, chapter XV, 388–89); see also Augustine, *Homilies on the Gospel of John*, John Gibb (trans) in Philip Schaff (ed) *Nicene and Post-Nicene Fathers*, vol. VII (Edinburgh: T&T Clark, 1991 [reprint]), tractate 99, sections 4–9, 382–84 and Hans Urs von Balthasar, *Theo-Drama: Theological Dramatic Theory*, volume V: *The Last Act*, Graham Harrison (trans) (San Francisco, CA: Ignatius Press, 1998), 245.

[46] Richard of St Victor, *The Trinity*, book 3, chapter XIV, 387–88.

[47] See Augustine, *The Trinity*, Edmund Hill, OP (trans) (Hyde Park, NY: New City Press, 1991), book 5, chapter 3, section 12, 197.

[48] The motif of the Father's womb, as formulated by the Council of Toledo in 675 CE, has been picked up by theologians like Balthasar, Moltmann (*The Trinity and the Kingdom*, 165), and Leonardo Boff (*Holy Trinity, Perfect Community*, 72) as a way to conceptualize non-patriarchal divine paternity. Balthasar emphasizes the emptiness of the Father's womb in *Theo-drama* vol. III, 518.

excessive procession of ecstatic love.[49] He is no human male whose capacity is exhausted in one final climax.

The Spirit, the Father's climactic emissary, hovers over the unformed waters, then shapes the transformation of the Son into the Father's seed, a seed which when cast into the ground makes the order of the world. But if reproduction belongs only to the Father within the trinity, the seed-Son cannot reproduce, and instead suffers castration (or the threat of castration) in order to become the "supra"-feminine space of the Father's self-enactment,[50] for the Son can do only what he sees the Father doing (John 5:19). If the Son participates in the procession of the Spirit, Father and Son together breathe out a sigh of union which turns tail and enfolds them both. The Son has then been given, not fatherhood, but potency—the ability to reproduce, or just to produce—in so transcendent a fashion that he does not even need to become father, for the law of the Father has been subjected to the law of the Son, who is begotten yet breathes and makes with no hint of his own sexuality. Perhaps the Spirit appears as the only true "man" (generic) in *this* image, for it is the Spirit alone who escapes sexual difference "in the name", and the Spirit who is not tied to anyone's apron strings as its indeterminacy frees it from full bondage in its originary site as the term of divine dependence.

In the missions, or their lived practice, these "utterly subjected" subjects "have no choice but to reiterate the law of their genesis."[51] That law is fulfilled economically when the Son hands the kingdom back to the Father so that God will be all in all (1. Cor. 15:28).[52] The distinctions among trinitarian persons are naturalized through the law of the Father. He is the originary origin, the one in whom all moments of difference find their beginning in his supreme, ultimate act of begetting, in which he shows the power of the divine nature by doing with it what he will, as Balthasar suggests.[53] This power of relational

---

[49] "Thus the Father causes the Son to be, to 'go'; but this also means that the Father 'lets go' of him, lets him go free. So too, in the act of begetting, a man causes his seed to go on its way while he himself retires into the background"; Balthasar, *Theo-drama* vol. V, 86. Marcella Althaus-Reid's apposite assessment of divine femininity may serve as a second epigraph for this argument: "What may worry us theologically is not necessarily what real phalluses may do, but the symbolic ones. What alarms us is not what role real clitorises fulfill, but the imaginary clitoris's function in the dialectics of membranous theologies (hymens) and life. . . . It may well be that God has a female sexuality without a clitoris, but with a hymen and a vagina for penetrative reproductive purposes, and this can then make the femininity of God irrelevant for women"; *Indecent Theology: Theological Perversions in Sex, Gender and Politics* (New York: Routledge, 2000), 73.

[50] Balthasar, *Theo-drama* vol. V, 91.

[51] Judith Butler, *Gender Trouble: Feminism and the Subversion of Identity* (New York: Routledge, 1999 [1990]), 135.

[52] See also Pannenberg, *Systematic Theology, Vol. 1*, 312–13 and Moltmann, *The Trinity and the Kingdom*, 91–2. Contrast Augustine, however, who emphasizes that Christ retains the kingdom as he hands it over to the Father, and that the Son has subjected all things to himself as well; *The Trinity*, book 1, chapter 3, sections 15–16, 75–6.

[53] Hans Urs von Balthasar, *Theo-Drama: Theological Dramatic Theory*, volume II: *Dramatis Personae: Man in God*, Graham Harrison (trans) (San Francisco, CA: Ignatius Press, 1990), 256. Cf.

self-disposal, identical with the Father's own being, generates a system of gift exchange within the trinity where the Son's reception of his being in gratitude turns into the enactment of submission and obedience.[54] The Spirit naturally and freely performs the distance and intimacy between the Father and the Son. Divine differentiation takes place through the eternal relations of origin in which God incessantly pours forth the fullness of differentiation into a tripartite movement of distinction in which the seeming destabilization of the natural relation between Father and Son through the Spirit (and in terms of divine gender) serves in truth to enact precisely the priority of that naturalized relationship. That is, the priority of the fatherhood of God, apparently displaced by the relation between him and his Son as it issues in the breathing out of their spiritual "child," is what is posited rather than destabilized by the seeming subversion of the system through the rejection of divine gender. Thus it is no wonder that the role of the Spirit in the economic life of the Son is to mediate to him "in the form of a rule" the will he once shared with the Father but to which he now must submit for a time as the temporal expression of his eucharistic gratitude to the Father. But the Son reasserts his own priority over the Spirit in the end.[55]

When the Son comes along, trapped in flesh thanks to the Spirit's whispering insinuation, the Spirit makes visible what no one else can see: hovering as a dove, this transcendent non-creature marks Jesus, while a voice speaks from heaven—"this is my beloved Son, in whom I am well pleased"[56]—showing that the lines of patriarchal inheritance remain intact, and that while the Father may have begotten a Word, he can still chatter. Yet the Spirit offers more. As the Son proceeds along his straight road to the cross, where does the Spirit go? At minimum, wherever he will: Jonathan Edwards says that the Spirit is "the principle that as it were reigns over the Godhead and governs his heart and wholly influences both the Father and the Son in all that they do."[57] The Spirit switches between sending and being sent, between topping and whispering, declaring and seducing. The Spirit comes at Pentecost in an unregulated outpouring that shocks the surrounding community, and intoxicates the disciples just enough that they declare their allegiance to the Son publicly. This happens just at the moment when the

---

also John Zizioulas's emphasis on the freedom with which the Father causes the Son and Spirit to exist. God "is Trinity not because the divine *nature* is ecstatic but because the Father as a *person* freely wills this communion"; *Being as Communion*, 44, emphasis in original; see also 41, 43 and *passim*.

[54] "In begetting the Son, the Father, as it were, addresses a request to him, and the Son in turn wishes nothing other than to employ his entire filial freedom in fulfilling the Father's will"; Balthasar, *Theo-drama* vol. V, 88.

[55] This is how Balthasar understands what he terms the "trinitarian inversion" in *Theo-drama* vol. III, 187–88.

[56] Matt. 3:17.

[57] Jonathan Edwards, "Discourse on the Trinity," *Works* volume 21, p. 147, quoted in Placher, *Triune God*, 100.

Son seems to be gone for good, not only because he has poured himself out on the cross but because even his ah!-so-penetrable post-resurrection body has gone away in its ascension to a higher heaven in which it sits at the right hand of the Father. Transformed into bread and wine, the disciples are now "biting and chomping"[58] on Jesus and, given courage and speech by the Spirit, they are able to speak of these things openly, without secrecy: coming out. And in their proclamation, propagated through faithful non-sexual reproduction over the centuries, they come to approach asymptotically the perfection of the Son's relation to the Father under the sign of the Spirit, adopted as "sons" identified by the perfection of their adherence to the form of the Father's originary power (speaking "begotten, not made").[59]

The Spirit, like the Son, leaves home. But while the Son finds himself utterly subjected—to the Father, to his desire for the world—the Spirit eventually gets to have all the fun. No one can predict (or predicate?) it. Sometimes it whispers—but did it not also storm and light fires? Those who are marked by the Spirit fall into an unregulated frenzy and behave in strange and unpredictable ways: "The Spirit's workings lie beyond control or prediction, but their effects are visible enough. They seize people, transforming them, making leaders of outsiders and reducing kings to comatose nakedness."[60] The enlivening Spirit-dove gets tossed out from the Father's hand and enters into the womb—the only member of the trinity who brushes against a woman? Or a form of artificial insemination, suggesting that on the human level, the Father is not as potent as he is divinely. Speaking from the Spirit's place denies the priority of inheritance and masculine generativity. Fire licking, hovering above disciples enlivened and transformed, speaking the word anew.

Starting from the Spirit

The recognition of Christianity's constitution as a logic of multiplicity rather than oneness in trinitarian doctrine is often a way to use an especially powerful or "orthodox" imagistic register to approach ends known to be desirable in advance of a detailed engagement with the material of trinitarian reflection, in structurally similar fashion to the delight with which other theologians "discover" that obedience and hierarchy need not entail inequality through examination of the relation between the Father and the Son. Both kinds of claims depend on successful depatriarchalization of the Father-God. But under the regime of sexuality's production of identity through insistence

---

[58] Marilyn McCord Adams, *Christ and Horrors* (Cambridge: Cambridge University Press, 2006), 310–11.

[59] See Virginia Burrus, *Begotten, Not Made: Conceiving Manhood in Late Antiquity* (Stanford, CA: Stanford University Press, 2000).

[60] William Placher, *Triune God*, 88. Similarly, "from the start, then, the Spirit can be helpful and life-giving but also unpredictable, uncontrollable, potentially terrifying" (86).

on sexual difference's constitutive status, we have reason to be suspicious both of the likelihood that a divine father *could be* so restricted and restrained, and of insistence that he *has been*—especially if the technical stipulations of trinitarian theology are either covered over or simply replaced (as is notoriously the case with Creator, Redeemer, and Sanctifier) without engagement with the theo-logics that generate such stipulations to begin with.

The problem is not ultimately that God is understood as father rather than, say, mother, or in the linguistic gendering of the divine; the problem lies more fundamentally in two alternative forms of telling and selling trinitarian histories. The first pretends that relating God the Father rightly to human fathers (through analogy and transcendence) and to the Son (through unsubstitutability and directing one's vision only to the Father of the Son) generates a Father unconnected to Christian patriarchies. Christianity's patriarchal history—which is not its only history!—is apparently made to disappear only to become more powerful through continued or even heightened insistence on the perfection and uniqueness of divine paternity in relation to contemporary forms of social organization.[61] The second takes the positive potential of the trinity as a resource for envisioning and valuing difference and multiplicity without engaging the trinity's particular and concrete histories of development and reflection, practicing renaming without undoing. The idol-skewering potential of skewed theological language is blunted (if not dropped altogether) in such moves.

Insofar as it is taken to be the "second difference," the Spirit cannot and will never hold open the relation between the Father and the Son in the way that some current projects require it to do. Considering the Spirit as the second difference or the Father as the first and the Son as the second person of the trinity, even if such construals are followed or accompanied by denial that number and its gendered correlate strictly speaking applies to the trinity, renders the Spirit a place, a site, for the becoming of the positive personalities of Father and Son and denies the immediacy and inseparability the trinitarian persons have in relation to each other. The more promising implication of the Spirit's positionality is that in its wildness and unpredictability, its priority in Christian experience, and perhaps most significantly, in that the Spirit has almost never been accused of begetting or generating another divine person, the Spirit's personhood can delineate a model for the theological transformations that Father and Son require. In this way, they too may undergo a successful operation of "re-skewing" so as to generate a more adequate trinitarian theology. But the Spirit cannot do this work alone. Reading the

---

[61] Note that when Aquinas justifies father-language for the Principle of the trinity, he does so in part because paternity is the "complement of generation," not due to any sort of analogy with (patriarchal or non-patriarchal) human fatherhood as a social practice. His justification may therefore not hold when it no longer becomes possible to see paternity in that way; *Summa Theologica* Ia, 33.2, ad. 2, 75.

trinity askew requires taking the terms of the revealed or creedal trinity with utmost seriousness, so seriously that the performance reveals the truth of the constitutive exclusions and failures of the trinitarian imaginary while enacting other possibilities of reading the history from which all trinitarian theology springs, the enactment of God-with-us and God-for-the-world in the life of Jesus and in the invisible, indeterminate, and potentially free presence of the Holy Spirit.

Reskewing trinitarian language, starting from the Spirit, has the potential to deregulate the Father and the Son from their subjected paternal-filial focus on each other. Setting the trinitarian imaginary free from its dogmatic and material connection to the fascination of Christian thought with the singularity of origin and origin's limited heritability opens the future of systematic theology to an outfolding movement beyond the antitheses of paternity, origination, and submission. This requires describing trinitarian distinctions without origin, either as fidelity to the origin of Christian speech of the trinitarian God or yet more significantly as origin-relations between divine persons. To speak "Father" without fatherhood sets the language of fatherhood askew in a yet more thorough-going fashion than the perfection of divine paternity in distinction to the failures and fractures of its human instantiation can achieve. Speaking improperly of the trinity—starting from the Spirit, without origin, and without the overdetermination of the Father and the Son as it is structured by the latter's grateful reception of the "gift" of divine being—reshapes the material of systematic theology without losing its genetic connection to the history of Christian thought. Trinitarian theology without origin requires no first, second, or third, the numeration of trinitarian persons that, despite stipulative denials, continues to reveal hierarchies denying the revelation of God in Christ and Spirit through their subjection, via origin, to the law and will of the Father. But the priority of the Spirit will not do much to transform the theological imaginary unless the Spirit's confrontation with the Father and the Son takes place face to face, without avoiding or eliding their material histories. Said more directly, without engagement with the technicalities of trinitarian theology on their own terms, the trinity will not be displaced as the site of the maintenance of the masculine divine. The Spirit neither begets nor generates. It escapes final signification. Its underdetermination must serve as a model for the other trinitarian persons.[62] Otherwise their masculinity will remain, even if it is

---

[62] This is *not* to say that the trinitarian persons should be rendered generic, nor to say that they need to be expanded to or identical with one another in a way that would threaten their real distinctions. The Spirit's freedom from originating another divine person ought, I am suggesting, to be expanded to the rest of the trinity, but distinction must remain. Relations of origin are not the only way in which divine persons may be distinguished. Epistemically, the economy of salvation requires an immanent distinction between the persons, but it does not demand a particular metaphysics of distinction. The tradition has occasionally flirted with other accounts of distinction (absolute persons or reciprocal constitution, for instance).

made invisible through insistence on the impossibility of divine gender, as long as origin-relations remain the referent of paternity and sonship in God. Reskewing the material registers of trinitarian language requires polyfidelity expressed through dual and simultaneous readings of the trinitarian imaginary in the conventional idiom of systematic theology and in recognition and analysis of the imagistic work done by the linguistic materialities that enliven trinitarian discourse. The different registers of trinitarian relations, sexual difference, and the difference beyond difference that names the God-world relation must be disconnected from each other and allowed their own separate integrities instead of projecting a more beautiful version of fatherhood into God. The motivation for such disconnection is fidelity to the truth of God-with-us in Christ and the Spirit. A polydox theology cannot limit its loves monolatrously.

Modern Theology 30:3 July 2014
ISSN 0266-7177 (Print)
ISSN 1468-0025 (Online)

DOI: 10.1111/moth.12122

RECEIVING THE GIFT

GRAHAM WARD

An Initial Question

How do I receive the gift of *Polydoxy: A Theology of Multiplicity and Relation?*[1] I will receive it, of course, in some way because simply by reading and absorbing the text, it will impact in some measure. I *am* affected by it; my mirror-neurones will ensure that. But just as in life we meet many different people and relate to them in various ways and with the majority of whom I will only form tangential and contingent relations, so too, though affected by this book, I might not be challenged by it (either positively or negatively). But then in not being challenged, in not being consciously affected and allowing myself consciously to be affected, then what I am receiving is not being received *as a gift*. And it is as a gift that I receive this book, and not simply because there are people who have contributed to it that I regard as friends (which is more than colleagues), people whose work and person I respect. So *how* do I receive this gift?

It is not an easy question to answer, and in fact my attempt at answering it is an exploration acknowledging its complexity. I accept and have myself attempted to think through theological transcorporeality, multiple belonging and the interpenetration of relations. And so the very "I" within the question is not a stable entity. The "I" is not only contextualised, it emerges from within the contextualisation and so its standpoint is evolving and shape-shifts. That does not mean that the "I" today is gone tomorrow. An identity for that "I" subsists. The experiences I have are *my* experiences. They cannot happen to someone else in an identical manner because I experience them through my singular embodiment and the history of that embodiment,

Graham Ward
Christ Church, St Aldate's, Oxford OX1 1DP, UK
Email: graham.ward@theology.ox.ac.uk

[1] Catherine Keller and Laurel C. Schneider (eds), *Polydoxy: Theology of Multiplicity and Relation* (New York: Routledge, 2011). Subsequent references to *Polydoxy* will be cited internally according to author, title and page number.

sedimented in a body that remembers far, far more than its cognitive capacity to remember. Any human being has multiple forms of memory. The question is further complicated by the fact that the book is composed not of one voice but twelve voices, each in their turn ventriloquizing other voices, like Deleuze's or Whitehead's. How is it possible then to receive all these voices, which share a common sensibility but not in any homogenous manner? I am not sure it is possible, and certainly not within the limited scope of one essay. And besides, not all the contributions affected me to the same degree; I engaged with some more than I did with others. There are degrees of engagement, as there are degrees of love, degrees of friendship. Not all relations are the same; each relation is registered singularly. My degree of engagement is not an evaluative judgement so much as recognition of certain folds of intensity between my own interests, desires, and questing and particular contributions. Other readers will respond differently both to the texts that drew me and to those that did not. These folds of intensity are the locations where I was able to receive the gift more profoundly and suffer the gift to be gift; for a gift has to be suffered if there is to be any genuine response that acknowledges the degree of its giftedness.

The First Cut

I want to begin to articulate my reception by recording a surprise; and surprise is one of the hallmarks of a gift. A gift, like love, is not deserved. It is not earned. It may be expected but not expected as part of an obligation to be met. The expectation is more a hope. So surprise is important. We have all learnt so much about our prejudgement now from hermeneutics and phenomenology; we project an anticipation of meaning. A characteristic of the surprise a genuine gift evokes is the way in which our prejudgments are thwarted, pleasantly and unpleasantly; unpleasantly because reception is a labour. To be able to dismiss an object because it confirms our prejudgement requires that we no longer have to undertake the labour of critical discernment. But the thwarting of our prejudgements can also be pleasant because something new is being offered and that incites curiosity. In the readjustment of our expectations we open ourselves to another expectancy—to an unknown, a new exploration of meaning.

I was surprised because from the title *Polydoxy* I anticipated some repristination of contemporary neo-paganism and the pop-transcendence of some amorphous spirituality that, to my mind, anaesthetises rather than enlightens because it cannot call forth the discipline of discernment. The solid melts, the substantial liquidises and there is so little to get hold of in a cosmic blancmange; so little that can help us; so little that can "save" us; so little that can get us to think and act in a world that is not one marvellous *sacra convivium*. It can't be when the throats of women and children are slit and their bodies left in dusty, Syrian streets. The world is heavily disturbed with the emanations of human violence; it reverberates with the screams and cries of grief and appalling loss, with indiscriminate and malicious violations. And some mysticisms are proffered that are cheap, only placebos for those who can afford to indulge them and forget. But *Polydoxy* did not conform to my expectations, certainly not in those locations where the folds of my engagement were most intense and demanded, as part of the reception, a labour to discern my response and the nature of the gift I was receiving.

If I begin then with a critical edge, it is not intended as a violent intervention, but more to sound the voice of the other, the difference that does not wish to separate and dismiss. It is an intervention that wishes to find a way of entering the web of communicative relations that composes the book and offers itself to the public. My intervention is a Christian one—while recognising the complex foldings within which Christianity finds itself and emerges historically with respect to Judaism and Islam and more recently with respect to Hinduism and Buddhism. It takes the form of two texts from the Christian Scriptures. Appealing to the Christian Scriptures makes my intervention a supplement because several contributors themselves have made similar appeals. Furthermore, any number of the contributors appeal to major writers within the Christian tradition—Tertullian, Irenaeus of Lyon, Augustine, Nicholas of Cusa, to name only a few—whose lives were interpellated in and through the Christian Scriptures. My intervention through the Scriptures is not simply supplementary, however, for it is raising a question about the roles of revealed truth and authority within polydoxy's project. Certainly the theologians from the Christian tradition I have named all regarded the Scriptures as authoritative, though the nature of that authority is complex and needs to be examined.

For the moment, let me consider two Christian Scriptural texts: The first is from the *Epistle of St. James*: "What is your life [*poia ē zōē umōn?*] For you are a mist [*atmis*] that appears for a little time and then vanishes [*pros oligon phainomenē . . . aphanizomenē*]" (James 4.14). The second is from the *Gospel of John*, when Christ, addressing his disciples, tells them, "No longer do I call you servants, for the servant does not know what his master is doing; but I have called you friends" (John 15.15).

James

The verse from the *Epistle of St. James* is interesting in part because it comes from a text in which the verb to make [*poieō*] and the noun [*poiesis*] are significantly associated with the divine. *Polydoxy* draws on the language of *theopoiesis* that took root in the Alexandrian Fathers. The author of the *Epistle* does not use the term, which Clement and Athanasius employed to describe how human being are "made God". But there is an emphasis in the letter upon creation and God's own *poieō*, and then a subsequent emphasis upon human beings participating in that divine making in its own way such that human beings are deified. The Alexandrian Fathers develop the participative ontology whereby human *poiesis in Christ* is enfolded in the operations of God in the world. Here in 4.14 the "you", which is plural, is identified with a singular "mist" (*atmis*)—the Greek word from which we get "atmosphere"—and, depending upon its translation, it can be associated with air and breath (as vapour) or with water (as steam) or with fire (as smoke). What is important is that it names a collection of first person singulars in a form that is permeable and continually morphing. Viewed as belonging to such an entity, James provides a figure for what Judith Butler, cited in Mary-Jane Rubenstein's contribution to the *Polydoxy* book, calls "a tenuous we" (Rubenstein, "Undone by each other: interrupted sovereignty in Augustine's *Confessions*," 105). The mist is a body, a material body, but it becomes impossible to make a decision about who is included or excluded from this body which may swell and contract in accord with the submission of its contingency to a brief span (*oligos*) between a fading in and a fading out. The poetry of the Greek lies in the liquid and soft consonants and the long vowels, the alliteration and the assonance. The whole of life is summed up in the slight transformation from the present participle in its deponent form of the verb *phaino* (to appear, become evident, coming to light) to the present passive participle of its opposite verb *aphanidzo* (to hide, remove, disappear). Notice the description is not a move from the present into the past; the transformation unfolds in the continuous present and will unfold while there is life at all. This unfolding, with its fade-ins and fade-outs of a tenuous we, *is* life. That is significant: it is not just a description of our lives, but also a definition of the essence of living itself.

Who then is the "you" to whom James is speaking? The author defines them as his "brethren" and the letter is addressed ambivalently to "the twelve tribes *in* (*en*) the dispersion" (James 1.1). These people hold the faith of our Lord Jesus Christ (2.1), are heirs to the promised kingdom (2.5), they believe that God is one (3.18) and they are awaiting the coming of the Lord (5.7). So this "mist" is composed of Christians, probably Jewish Christians because of the continual references to Jewish biblical figures and the law, divided into "twelve tribes" and dispersed across a multiplicity of locations and in a multiplicity of races. The belonging (which is a word I wish to return to) here, within and as the mist, is complex and probably mirrors the complex relations (of gender, race, class and past religious adherences) that identified themselves as churches in specific geographical locations in the early centuries of Christianity.

Paul

If the author of the *Letter to the Ephesians* (which is disputably Paul) is right, then what associated the complex relations of church in one place with the complex relations of church in another place was "one [*mia*] hope that belongs to your call, one [*eis*] Lord, one [*mia*] faith, one [*en*] baptism" (Eph. 4.5). And it is this commonality that constituted "one [*en*] body and one [*en*] Spirit". This one body and one spirit is called into being and the origin of that calling is "one [*eis*] God and Father of us all, who is above all and through all and in all" (Eph. 4.6). Oneness here, whether of the body, the spirit or God, does not mean homogeneity. In fact, the very repetition of "one" elides different understandings of oneness. Okay, the change in Greek between *eis, mia* and *en* is in accord with the gender of the noun. But the oneness of the body is composed of its operational parts; oneness here is a close synonym for the Whole. The oneness of the Spirit is its singularity, the Holy Spirit of Eph. 1.13, elsewhere the Spirit of Christ. Similarly, the oneness of the Lord is also a singularity, the historical singularity of Jesus the Christ (Eph. 1.3). The oneness of hope names the consensus of Christian conviction in the Christ event, as does the oneness of faith. It is the single, agreed and experienced orientation of those who have been called. The oneness of baptism names that inaugural liturgical event whereby each person is initiated into being a member of the church; the repetition of the same sacramental act. This is a oneness which is not one and the changes in Greek adjective, although merely lexical, do help to suggest what Catherine Keller, citing Laurel C. Schneider, draws our attention to in her contribution to the *Polydoxy* volume: "Different not separate; distinct not divided" (Keller, "Be a multiplicity: ancestral anticipations," 94). The repetition of "one" is neither univocal nor equivocal; it is analogical.

Let me take this argument one step further because it will relate to a later exposition of the participative ontology of relations which polydoxy advocates and its similarities to and differences from the Johannine emphasis upon friendship and the intercorporeality expressed in phrases like, "that they may be one [*en*]; even as thou, Father, art in [*en*] me, and I in [*en*] thee, that they may be in [*en*] us" (John 17.21). We can even pick up that oneness again with this verse. For the oneness even here is complex, multiple, and folds into itself paradoxically. Of course there is a difference between the number one [*en*] and the use of the locational dative in [*en*], but the repetition of this same Greek syllable articulates the slips and elisions involved in what a number of contributors to *Polydoxy*, drawing upon Laurel Schneider's work, term "the logic of the One". If there is a logic of oneness expressed in this verse, it is not a human logic (other than perhaps the logic of an Escher drawing). The pronouns, and therefore the subjects, "they", "you" and "I" are neither negated nor dissolved but coexist within each other. What is being expressed here is a theo-logic that cannot be fully understood or explicated: a being one in a way that is not being one as we understand and employ the word and yet because God's revelation of Godself in and as creation is an accommodation to our creatureliness, the oneness expressed says something about oneness as it pertains to the Godhead. But a profound, learned ignorance has to be confessed about what oneness is with respect to God; we do not know what we are saying even when confessing *credo in unum deo*. As John Thatamanil points out in his contribution, "God as ground, contingency, and relation": "remember the warning of the Fathers that number cannot mean in the divine life what it means in quotidian experience. Only finite realities can be enumerated; the infinite cannot. Neither one nor three can mean for the divine life what numbers mean in conventional experience" (Thatamanil, "God as ground, contingency, and relation," 240). There can be there a "logic of the One" which is far from being tyrannical. Analogy, the use human language to express divine realities, does not span the difference between God's creator being and our derived being; it expresses a greater dissimilarity than similarity. Nevertheless, the difference does not establish an untransgressable ontological divide. If there were such a divide then there could be no incarnation and, as Wittgenstein said famously of lions, if God spoke we could know nothing about it.

The analogical nature of oneness is summed up in that mellifluous line, "one [*eis*] God and Father of us all, who is above all and through all and in all [*o epi pantōn kai dia pantōn kai en pansin*]" (Eph. 4.6). More accurately, there is no "us" in the Greek, as there is in the English translation, and there is no verb either (which means the "is" is not in the Greek: God and Father of all). I want to read this phrase as I believe and will argue it should be read, in part on the basis that there is no verb. The three substantive nouns—God, Father and the pronoun "who"—are constantive. Fatherhood is not then a divine attribute. The word "fatherhood" is, of course, gendered, because that is the nature of the Greek language (and the French, and the German language etc.)—though it could legitimately be translated "founder". But what I suggest is that the distinctive syntax of the phrase suggests it should be read not descriptively (that would accept fatherhood as an attribute), but rather prescriptively: that is, as a rule for the employment of the word "God" by Christians in a Hellenistic culture saturated with references to *theos, theoi, thea* and *theaina*. In other words, the phrase is telling us how Christians use the word *theos* and understand the adjective oneness with respect to this *theos*. "God" means "that author or progenitor of all". *Theos*, and how it should be used and understood among Christians, is then further defined by the clause that follows "the one who is above (*epi*) all that was brought into being, the one who governs all movement and operations within (*dia*) all that was brought into being, and the one who permeates the material specificity (*en*) of all that was brought into being." "God" as the word is defined for Christian usage does not then announce a simple panentheism. The word expresses the nature of a Creator who is more than just in (*en*) all. If "polydoxy" "does not fold orthodoxy down; it *complicates* it" (Keller and Schneider, "Introduction," 8), then maybe orthodoxy is actually already more complicated than polydoxy gives it credit for. I don't wish to rush here into labelling my exegesis of a Christian Scripture as "orthodox"; a number of questions are left begging here and we need to approach them in an orderly way. What I just wish to point out is that the second phrase defining how Christians should use and understand the word *theos* opens by situating God as "above" (*epi*) all things and that it is only in being above all things that we can proceed to define this God as the operative dynamic within (*dia*) all things which then leads to the conclusion that this God must be in (*en*) all things.

Why do we need the *epi* and the *dia* before we arrive at the *en*? Just two points: first, because the Christian term *theos* refers neither to the sum of all things (which would be the pantheism of some of the Presocratics and some of the Stoics) nor simply the unfolding, animating process in all things (which would be the panentheism of some middle-Platonists). The Christian term *theos* refers to the Creator who by being above all things governs their unfolding and because of this a distance (the *distema* that is so characteristic of apophaticism in the Greek Fathers) always prevails between the one who creates and all things created. The distance does not constitute a difference that separates, but it does announce an asymmetrical relation between creator and created. It is this asymmetrical relation that governs analogical predication. Concerning that government, God's providential operations through time and place and persons, we have to admit a healthy agnosticism. Certainly that government could not be so neatly described as "unilateral control over the world's becoming" (Hartung, "Faith and polydoxy in the whirlwind," 154), because each noun and adverb in that phrase presumes access to a knowledge of the divine nature which we possess only in a mirror darkened by our own desires and limitations. Secondly, we need the *epi* and the *dia* before we arrive at the *en* because while I wish to agree wholeheartedly with Mayra Rivera's beautiful depictions of "a universe inherently marked by the divine mystery" (Rivera, "Glory: the first passion of theology?" 178), "the scintillating opacity of carnality and materiality, and . . . their indefinite complexity" (Rivera, "Glory," 179) and that the manifestation of God's glory "is never outside materializations" (Rivera, "Glory," 180), the danger here is to collapse a difference between nature and grace. God's glory is never outside materialization *for we* who are creaturely. But there is a glory "above" and it is by means of that "above" that there can be a "through" and an "in". To collapse the difference between grace and nature (and the difference again never constitutes a dualism) has two immediate corollaries: there is no longer any gift because, at best, this is a matter of divine and necessary emanation; and there is no distinction between revelation (of the Creator within creation) and disclosure or, in Nancy's terms "dis-enclosure".[2] For Nancy, as I read him, follows a trajectory opened by Lyotard, of a sublime and unpresentable in the world disclosed by the world on a plane of immanence. This is not how Christians have traditionally understood the nature of revelation as God's manifestation of Godself in the world that, for Christians, is always a revela-

---

[2] See J.-L. Nancy, *Dis-Enclosure: The Deconstruction of Christianity*, B. Berge *et.al.* (trans) (New York: Fordham University Press, 2008).

tion of Christ. Now, let me be clear, I do not wish to make a dualistic distinction between revelation and disclosure, just as I do not wish to make a dualistic distinction between grace and nature. Taking aesthetic appreciation as a model for disclosure and the transfiguration of the ordinary, there are disclosive moments in novels and poetry, for example, which I have argued elsewhere challenge any view of the secularisation of modern literature.[3] In fact, I understand poetry as not particularly trying to say something specific but exploring the invisible as it clings to the visible as and in language. There are writers like Flannery O'Connor and Graham Greene who have closely associated this disclosive effect with the revelation of God, in ways highly sophisticated, nuanced, weighted with theological ambiguity and complexity.[4] Nevertheless, the maintenance of an *epi* and a *dia* with respect to the operations of God in the world enjoins a difference but not separation between revelation and disclosure.

At this point it is worth complicating my own analysis. I have claimed and argued that the Christian use and understanding of *theos* cannot announce a simple panentheism; but what about an "apophatic panentheism" (Keller, "Be a multiplicity," 101, n. 84)? Apophasis, along with a series of other terms with a negative suffix (like infinite, analogy and impassable), assists in clarifying what we can and what we cannot say accurately with respect to the term *theos*, and therefore what we can and what we cannot understand about God. It refers to an unsaying. Apophasis is not agnosticism, the ambivalence of undecideability or indeterminacy, the name for an abyssal aporia or the name of the gaps in what sub-atomic physics on the nature of materiality and neuroscience on the nature of mind cannot yet plug with explanations. Neither is it mystery in terms of some darkness within which God hides Godself. God does not hide Godself—the gift of Godself is given absolutely and eternally. In the words of Mayra Rivera, which I completely support: "Incomprehension remains in revelation, not because some knowledge is kept hidden but because knowledge is never fully adequate for the glory's significance" (Rivera, "Glory," 177)—though I would add that I do not interpret Nancy's "dis-enclosure" as saying the same thing when she extends her analysis in footnote 54 of her contribution. Apophasis is the result of our creaturely limitations in which the knowledge of God that we articulate self-consciously deconstructs itself. We do not employ apophatic discourse in order to safeguard God's holy distinctiveness, but rather to regulate our God-talk *for our sake*—because to claim more than can be claimed or inferred from what can be claimed, to fly off into mystical speculations, doesn't help

---

[3] Graham Ward, "How Literature Resists Secularity", *Literature and Theology*, Vol. 24. no.1 (2010), 73–88.
[4] Of the works of Flannery O'Connor see the novel, *The Violent Bear It Away* (New York: Farrer, Straus and Giroux, 1955) and for Graham Greene see the novel *The Power and The Glory* (London: Vintage, 2004).

"save" us. At its most benign it is just escapism; at its most malign it can constitute a delusive ideology that will only perpetrate those violences I spoke of earlier. But, as an adjective qualifying panentheism, what is the object of that admission of a "learned ignorance"? Surely, it can only be that "en," that indwelling of the divine within "all things". So the question becomes: does the apophasis concern *how* God dwells within all things, the nature of God *in* the divine indwelling of all things, or both? As one marker which describes God-with-us in a way that refutes hierarchical dualisms such as transcendence over immanence, divine grace over nature, and affirms the incarnation of the divine, then panentheism is helpful and apophatic panentheism would remind us of a restricted understanding of the nature of God in God's divine indwelling. That is, a difference between our knowledge of the immanent and eternal trinity and our attempts to grapple with the effects of the temporal operations of the economic trinity. But we do have knowledge of *how* God indwells within all things that is not apophatic. It may never be a perfect knowledge but there is the knowledge of being called that the verse from *Ephesians* speaks of. There is knowledge of a divine election, a divine governance or providence, a process of sanctification, the kingdom that is coming, human sin and its redemption. We have knowledge above all on the basis of the incarnation of God in time and place. We have knowledge then of God's economic operations in the world that allows us to use cataphatic discourse on the basis of the life, work and teachings of Jesus Christ as God. But, and this is the point—and a point that returns to the question of revelation and Scriptural authority—it is a knowledge on the basis of faith; faith in the articles of the Christian faith distilled by the church over decades of discernment from the Scriptures and summed up in the creeds. And "faith is the assurance of things hoped for, the conviction of things not seen" (Hebrews 11.1). It is certainly not "a simple access to certainty" (Hartung, "Faith and polydoxy in the whirlwind," 151); it is quite definitely and necessarily open, vulnerable and blind. Faith is a suffering in the same way that continuing to "hope . . . against hope" (Rom. 4.18) demands more from us than despair. Faith is not about making assertions; it is a courageous groping towards promises in Christ that may or may not have been understood. So, sharpening my question even further, does the adjective "apophatic" when associated with panentheism name a certain theological investigation which accepts God's indwelling of creation, and examines that indwelling in terms of evolutionary biology, quantum mechanics, mathematics and the theory of multiplicity while rejecting the foundation of the Christian faith that God has revealed Godself in Jesus Christ and the Christian Scriptures which participate in some very complex manner in that revelation? Does apophasis creep into the gap left when the call to and substance of the Christian faith is dissolved? Is the apophatic, then, in "apopathic panentheism" equivalent to the "ambiguous" in Colleen Hartung's claim: "divine occurrence is known within or as ambiguous bodily experience"

(Hartung, "Faith and polydoxy in the whirlwind," 154). If the answers to these last questions are yes, then this is a transferred, even metaphorical use of *apophasis* as it is employed and understood in the context of the Christian tradition.

Anne

One of the most significant encounters I had in reading *Polydoxy* was engaging with the work of Anne Conway. I had never heard of her before and from the account of her work in Catherine Keller's contribution she was undoubtedly a prescient and subtle theological thinker. I concur with Conway's examination of "the free interactivities" (Keller, "Be a multiplicity," 92) of all created things, our "intercreaturely evolution" (Keller, "Be a multiplicity," 93) and "the Emanations of one Creature into another" (Keller, "Be a multiplicity," 92). I also concur that this is an account of God's indwelling in creation and therefore a description of divine operations in, through and across all the bodies that compose an always-in-process and intricately complex world-order. But, as Anne Conway seemed to have appreciated, this is not an account of God in Godself, what the Christian understands by the term "God" as Creator of all things, above all things and therefore exterior, anterior and posterior to creation. It is an account of the infinite web of relations established by God in creating and sustaining that creation. Orthodoxy (if that is what we want to call it; I would go for something a little looser like "the Christian faith seeking understanding") in wishing both to discern and be obedient to the truth revealed in Christ and attested to in the Scriptures, is a great deal more complicated than a doctrine of creation. The complexity of creaturely multiplicity multiplies. And perhaps I need to add here that the doctrines of the Christian faith are not propositional truths. There are no "doctrinal certainties" (Hartung, "Faith and polydoxy in the whirlwind," 151) in the positivist understanding of either a propositional truth claim or a certainty. The doctrines of the faith, endlessly being formulated and reformulated, constitute a grammar for the production of the Christian talk about God. So that when the claim is made that Jesus was a man adopted by God then such a claim is registered as ungrammatical, i.e., that is not the way the Christian faith parses the relationship between "Jesus", "man" and "God". Furthermore, in distorting the grammar of Christology in this way there are chains of implications for other doctrines articulated: of God, of salvation, of the church, of creation, etc. It is important to understand what is at stake here because it is not a matter of marking this Christological articulation wrong in an essay or even shouting an anathema. A Christology so articulated cannot do what it is said and believed that Christ did: come into the world to redeem the human condition. On this Christological articulation there can be no human assumption into the Godhead; God indwells creation along the dualistic model of a divine ghost in a human machine; creation is ontologically divided from the Godhead; it is not a *sacramentum mundi*; the church cannot be the body of Christ, etc., etc. Work on Christian doctrines, in systematic theology, is not about creating certainties or proving things to be the case; its concern is whether talk about God can adequately attest to the work God came into the world in Christ to perform. If God-talk cannot adequately attest to this, then it is unhelpful for the church and for individual Christians in the ongoing process of discerning the truth that faith seeks to understand.

It is through this endless formulation and reformulation of the doctrines of Christian faith seeking understanding that any orthodoxy is *made*—as an important collection of essays edited by Rowan Williams argued convincingly.[5] Orthodoxy is not a monolithic given. It is not even an object. It is much better understood as an ongoing set of interrelated activities as Christian faith seeks understanding of the articles which compose that faith. It names a process begun with the revelation of God in Jesus Christ and only completed when time and creation itself come to their completion and all things are enfolded within the Kingdom; a process of discernment with respect to that revelation. It is inextricably bound to politics—cultural politics, party politics, the politics of competing sovereignties and ways human beings have shaped for governing themselves; but then we are as creatures political animals. When it stops being a process of discernment and it starts being an ideology then orthodoxy is reified; and reification is always possible and, when it occurs, always dangerous. My question is whether "polydoxy" is working with a reified understanding of "orthodoxy" in order to construct a position from which to announce its own distinctiveness? Orthodoxy is not a finished project; it is an emerging phenomenon—emerging from the various interconnected sites where the discernment process takes place. As several contributors remarked, *orthos* means "right", "just" even "straightforward". I view liberation theology's *orthopraxis* as a desire to pursue "right relations" and understand truth, goodness, justice and beauty, which are the allusive goals of those "right relations", not as substantives but emergent conditions or states of being. We will only know them to the extent we live them, that is, participate in and make them emerge. But there are questions here concerning the arenas within which the discernment process and pursuit of truth, goodness, justice and beauty take place. There are questions concerning the orders of interpellation or discipline within these arenas and authority.

John

To identify the issues more clearly here allow me to turn to the second text from John's Gospel, which clarifies "right relations". This is important, not least because polydox theology quite rightly to my mind emphasises that

---

[5] Rowan Williams (ed), *The Making of Orthodoxy: Essay in Honour of Henry Chadwick* (Cambridge: Cambridge University Press, 1989).

incarnation is inseparable from relationality. Furthermore, for Monica E. Coleman, the soteriology that issues from such relationality is inseparable from "lived communities of faith" (Coleman, "Invoking oya," 186). "No longer do I call you servants, for the servant does not know what his master is doing; but I have called you friends" (John 15.15). From later in this farewell discourse by Jesus to his disciples I have already outlined the concern with not just interelationality but intercorporeality in which the many (the disciples) are folded into Christ and Christ into God. The Pauline theology of the church as the body of Christ and the lived community of faith in the *First Letter to the Corinthians* expounds this intercorporeality further. At this point I only wish to make two observations. The first is Christological: the right relations are governed by discipleship, the logic and pedagogy of following Christ. Soteriology, which is never a matter of the individual, for the individual as such is incorporated in the multiplicity of Christ's body, proceeds through and in this discipleship. This returns us to a point I made above concerning systematic theology: in seeking to understand the nature and work of Christ, the Christological model for that nature and work has to be able to deliver the "salvation" promised by God. And salvation here I would relate directly to the Latin *salus*, where it means health and well being, though, governed as it is by an eschatology, that final health and well being is the resurrection of the body. A docetic Christological model, an Apollonian Christological model, even a kenotic Christological model along the lines of certain readings of Hegel, cannot deliver the salvation promised and summed up by any number of Church Fathers in terms of God becoming human so that the human might become deified. Only a Christ who is fully God and fully human can assume all that is human and return it to the divine. "To assert that God gives something other or less than Godself in giving Word and Spirit imperils salvation," as John Thatamanil states (Thatamanil, "God as ground, contingency, and relation," 238). The kenotic model conceived by certain interpreters of Hegel, for example, conflates Christ with creation, divinizing creation by rendering creation an emanation of the divine and conflating transcendence and immanence. Conflation is *not* the maintenance of difference without separation, but, in John Thatamanil's felicitous phrase, "undifferentiated simplicity" (Thatamanil, "God as ground . . . ," 238). Now if that kenotic Christology is deemed heterodox it is because it cannot "save" us. It cannot articulate the logic of the work Christ came to do. It is ungrammatical. Why can't such a model "save" us? First: because God would then need us to save Godself. Not a bad idea, some might say. But then that is not "God" as Christians have understood the word "God", contingent being is conflated with necessary being, and the temporal with the eternal. If we wish to maintain an ontological difference that is not a separation between God as Creator and us creatures, if we wish to maintain God who is eternal and the temporal order of creation, then such a conception of God who needs to be saved through us, through creation, is not the fount of endless, gracious love but a total tyrant; for creation is then only a by-product of such a God's coming to be God, of God's own self-determination. Creatureliness merely provides the host bodies for God becoming God. There are certain models of DNA, by Richard Dawkins for example, which suggest a similar condition: it is DNA that evolves and transmutes, creation at present is just the most adequate form for the survival of the genes.[6] Secondly, such a conception of God makes creation eternal, which is neither a Jewish, Christian nor Islamic teaching, and salvation is then merely a matter of what you get or don't get in this world. But the Christian promise, given through the resurrection of Christ, is that those who follow faithfully will be likewise resurrected. Eternal life is not now, the eschaton is not yet realised; eternal life is what Christians come into when the Kingdom is fully come. Thirdly, if God needs creation to become God and creation in being divinized becomes eternal, then sin (which was the reason for the incarnation of God) is not dealt with and judgement is not given. So the endless circles of human violence, the endless exercise of *libido dominandi*, continue. Such a conception of God requires a philosophy of history, history very much along the lines of Hegel's lectures on the philosophy of history, and if sin is being dealt with such history is committed to an ameliorative teleological progress. I am still unclear where process thought's commitment to "creative transformation" (Coleman, "Invoking oya," 189) sits with respect to the teleology of such a progress. I can envisage the coming of Christ as a sort of dose of antibiotics given to the body of creation and the emergence of pockets of right relations, which operate to transform the health of the whole. But such a utopian view of either history or creation is not biblical and would still have to reckon with the more apocalyptic readings of creation and history if it were to accord with Christian eschatology and the so-called last things. Neither does it sit easily with any physical science account of entropy. The idea of multiple saviours, each as leaders of their own local communities (Coleman, "Invoking oya," 190), is both a recipe for social fragmentation (which greatly qualifies the universalism of interrelationality and intercorporeality constituting a social ontology) and an acceptance that only local salvation is possible. What happens outside these communities to the rest of the world? Certainly when Hegel himself tried to compose a narrative of such creative transformation in history it required a full acceptance of what even he found some difficulty with—the atrocities perpetrated in the Reign of Terror following the French Revolution. It required evil as a dialectical necessity and figured history as a slaughterbench. We would have to accept similar and even more appalling atrocities in the progress of world history. Only a God who created us in and out of love and a Christ who is the incarnation of that God, and a Holy Spirit as completing and proceeding from that triune love can judge sin, know where it is to be found, and, in dealing with that sin, forgive, absolve.

---

[6] See Richard Dawkins, *The Selfish Gene* (Oxford: Oxford University Press, 1989).

Key to the materialization of that forgiveness in creation (which is also the healing of relations), key to the operation of divine love in, through and across our interrelationalities and intercorporealities, is friendship that binds together those "communities of living faith." Friendship is a gift; it is the very bond of belonging. It is bestowed upon Christians in and through Christ when he announces "I have called [*eirēka*] you friends." We observed above with respect to the *Letter to the Ephesians* the grace that is given in being called to Christ, but discipleship is a collective phenomenon for we are *called* to be in relation. While some Protestant theologies have emphasised this calling in terms of a doctrine of the election and predestination of the selected, theologies constructed around a Logos Christology have recognised the call to, in and as Christ as God's verbalisation of the Godhead in creation. As such the call is available to all, as the gift is available to all; though there remains the question of being able to hear and receive the call of Christ that corresponds directly with our God-given freedom. The call is to participation in God's triune love, here in the Gospel of John conceived as friendship. *Philos* had such a wide remit within Hellenistic culture, spanning friend, companion, lover, even married partner (usually husband). Homer defines Achilles as Patroclus' *periphilētos*—his greatly beloved. Friendship also allows for a variety of degrees of association, for the intensities, the collegialities, and the range of acquaintance that characterises interrelationality; for no relation is the same and all the affective registers of relations are subject to change. There is again a multiplicity of possibilities of relation here but they are governed Christologically; they belong to and in Christ. It might be said that all the relationalities are expressions and manifestations of a Christic indwelling. The church emerges within and as these sets of right relations, and therefore there is always a question of the relationship between this emerging church (the pilgrim church, as Augustine called it) and the institutional church. The latter cannot police the boundaries of the former, even if it wished to. Christ is performed in and through and as these right relations in which God as Spirit prevails. That is the nature of belonging.

If I have laboured the Christological issues it is because I have yet to have a sense of the Christological model polydoxy is presenting *and* to highlight that not all Christological models are possible. So choices in the multiplicity have to be made. And if a certain orthodoxy is manifest in this choosing it is not because orthodoxy itself imposes such a model (orthodoxy, as I have emphasised is made and is continually being made as Christian faith seeks understanding), but because the models rejected cannot offer a logic for our salvation.

An Inconclusive Conclusion

So putting aside the question of whether polydoxy isn't an artificial construction founded upon a certain reification of orthodoxy in the "logic of the One", can polydoxy save us? That's my real question, the question I have returned to in engaging with the various contributions to this collection (some more than others). In a sense to receive the gift of *Polydoxy: Theology of Multiplicity and Relation* and respond to it as a gift is already to have advanced and participated in the polydoxical. One adds one's voice to the multiplicity, a voice that rehearses and recites other voices, though modulated sometimes in more minor rather than major keys. Until, perhaps, the world is recognised as one vast and undulating field of communicative relations rather like the polyphonic music of Ainur that brought all things into being in the opening chapter of Tolkien's *Silmarillion*. What is it in such a polyphony that disturbs me as a Christian? From within the music of Ainur, it will be recalled, a violence and a strife emerged sending a tremor "into the silences yet unmoved." Perhaps, and this is the hazard theological discourse runs, I am disturbed because the aesthetic can so easily become the anaesthetic. *Polydoxy* as a volume ends on the word "vision", and I do not want to deny the vision, and the desire for transformation that drives the vision and informs the vision. But vision is not enough. Vision can spin fine words and it needs to engender fine actions. So to whom is this polydoxical vision addressed? What communities of lived Christian faith is it speaking to and attempting to inspire? Or is all this liberal academic good intentionalism? I write at the time in Britain when the newspapers herald on their front pages the celebration of gold laden Olympiads and the continuing devastation of Syria while a tooth-less UN looks on. Interrelationality, intercorporeality, social ontology—I belong to these two jarringly conflictual situations. So maybe what disturbs me is that talk about transformation and mutuality can come cheap for theologians: we need to hear the pain of the irreconcilable, acknowledge the rawness of the unforgiveable. There are astonishing depths of hatred, anguish, fear and impotence all around us and even within us, internalised. Multiplicity embraces a multitude of sins and sinners and sinned against. And there is that about the scandalous particularity of the crucified Christ that tells us something about the profundity of sin and the appalling cost of judgement. The resurrection, redemption and the Kingdom are hopes against hope and gifts of an unutterable grace. The polyphonic music of Ainur when disturbed by the inventions of Melkor is silenced by Ilúvatar who, in addressing Melkor, tells him: thou "shalt see that no theme may be played that hath not its uttermost source in me, nor can any alter the music in my despite. For he that attempteth this shall prove but mine instrument in the devising of things more wonderful, which he himself hath not imagined." So maybe in responding to this polydoxic gift I am playing the part of Melkor here.

Modern Theology 30:3 July 2014
ISSN 0266-7177 (Print)
ISSN 1468-0025 (Online)

DOI: 10.1111/moth.12123

WRITING-TERRORS: A DIALECTICAL LYRIC

MARK D. JORDAN

There is a reliable supply of books on method in Christian theology, but we writers of theology lack others that we need more urgently. We need books intended for those who come late in a theological tradition that long ago professed apophasis, but mostly relished imperial adventures. Fully aware of the risks of writing, needing from the first to excuse their own audacity—to justify the mere fact of their existence, these rarer texts encourage their readers towards artful composition by performing it.

I want to read at least some parts of the anthology entitled *Polydoxy* into this deliberate and historically alert genre.[1] I take as my guide the essay by Mayra Rivera Rivera.[2]

Praise of Terror

1. "Polydoxy" is a word recently assembled from Greek parts in reply to our meaning of "orthodoxy." "Polydoxy" was also a Greek word. In late ancient authors, it means something like a diversity of opinion. A related form applies to someone who holds various opinions. Of course, the old ambivalence of the root word "doxa" is preserved in its compounds: "polydoxized" (*poludoxastos*) means much praised.[3]

Mark D. Jordan
Harvard Divinity School, 45 Francis Avenue, Cambridge, MA 02138, USA
Email: mdjordan@wustl.edu

[1] Catherine Keller and Laurel C. Schneider (eds), *Polydoxy: Theology of Multiplicity and Relation* (London and New York: Routledge, 2011). Subsequent references to *Polydoxy* will be cited internally by author, essay title and page number.

[2] Mayra Rivera Rivera, "Glory: The First Passion of Theology?," in *Polydoxy*, 167–85.

[3] I am only paraphrasing part of the entry in H. G. Liddell and R. Scott, *Greek-English Lexicon*, ninth edition with a revised supplement (Oxford: Clarendon Press, 1996), at 1438a. For comments by several authors in the anthology on the multiple meanings of the root "doxa," see

One old meaning of "orthodoxy" in Christianity is not right opinion, but rightful praising. Many Eastern Christians still claim the word as a boast about their liturgies—or they remember that creeds were elements in public worship before they were party platforms.

Let polydoxy mean much praising.[4] Who is being praised? So far as polydoxy is theology, the obvious candidate would be a God or gods. So far as polydoxy is recognizable (in part) as Christian theology, this God would be the one to whom Jesus of Nazareth prayed.

2. What do I do when I praise his God? It can feel like the expression of feelings I have (or ought to have), but praise once spoken encourages, instructs, persuades others. Praising God aloud, I describe God and invite others to agree, to join in or join up.

Or perhaps my praise shows that I have stopped searching for positive descriptions of God. In the texts written under the pseudonym, "Dionysus the Areopagite," praise is what remains of theological speech under apophasis. The stripping away of divine attributes in his *Mystical Theology* is framed as prayer. It begins with a Trinitarian invocation. It ends in the rhythms of adoration, even as it forsakes every predication. The traditional arrangement of the Dionysian corpus shows the same transit through negation to praise. After the breathless end of *Mystical Theology*, the reader finds detailed encomiums of the two hierarchies by which God is reflected and worshiped—one celestial, the other ecclesiastical. In these texts, sequences of glorification trace the cosmic order.

Or perhaps my praise does not so much abandon description as fulfill its aims unexpectedly by action—by a sort of mime. God intends creatures for praise, so praise becomes their most accurate rendering of God. A creature describes God best by becoming the praise that God allots to it.

3. If all creatures exist by glorifying, then so do creatures of flesh and blood, vulnerable to the quick violence of assault and the slow violence of degradation. Saying that, I realize that I was being carried into theological fantasy by the flow of traditional language about divine intentions. One fantasy favored by Christian theology is a sort of hyperbole, a trope of excessive praise. Theology strives to exalt God by forgetting or falsifying creation.

In her essay for *Polydoxy* (2011), Mayra Rivera Rivera contrasts fantastical notions of praise with the cry of the oppressed. "The cry of injustice weighs

---

Polydoxy, 3, 168–69. Elsewhere, Whitehead's related coinages are mentioned as a precedent (an authorization?) for "polydoxy" (ibid., 6).

[4] This way of turning the etymology is suggested by several authors in *Polydoxy*, including Faber, "The Sense of Peace: A Para-Doxology of Divine Multiplicity" (36), and Rubenstein, "Undone By Each Other: Interrupted Sovereignty in Augustine's *Confessions*" (111, 121–23).

heavily on any thought of wonder and glory."[5] But that cry can also give to theological thinking the complication of truth. "Beauty and sensible pleasure are intrinsic to glory's lure. Yet glory is not simply another name for the beautiful; terror also arises from its encounter."[6] Glorifying God requires a response at once to beauty and to terror. In daily prayers, the psalm repeats: the beginning of wisdom is *fear* of the Lord (Ps. 111:10).

4. In glorifying God, the terror to be represented is not some Kantian sublime. It is more familiar and nauseating terror—the terror of human lives destroyed or human bodies mangled. How can that terror figure in the language of praise? How does it figure in language at all?

Michel Foucault's *Discipline and Punish* opens with a gore-splattered narration of the public torture of Robert-François Damiens, a rebellious servant condemned in 1757 for attempting to assassinate King Louis XV. Readers recall these infamous pages as spoken in Foucault's voice, as his close paraphrase of selected sources. But Foucault begins his book in fact with a string of quotations. The first twelve paragraphs consist almost entirely of excerpts from archived texts: published trial proceedings, a newspaper account, firsthand testimony by a police official. Foucault writes in them only introductory or linking phrases and ellipses.[7]

A squeamish reader, I would prefer to skip over these excerpts. That is one of Foucault's reasons for including them. He means for modern readers to find them revolting, barbaric, and (above all) *medieval*. He expects that I will feel a sense of relief when I pass from such gruesome testimonies to a modern list of penal prescriptions. One aim of *Discipline and Punish* is to examine my relief on reaching my own society's networks of incarceration—which are not for punishment, of course, but for rehabilitation. Of course!

5. There is something else—in my squeamishness, in Foucault's quotations. There is the act of *writing down* terror. What practice of writing is it that can be content to describe a body being ripped apart under royal authority, in the presence of Christian ministers?

If I wish (impossibly) to protect language from such abuses, I wish even more that such texts not result from any act of religious writing. Yet Foucault insists not only that language regularly serves terror, but that these particular texts are a species of theology—doxology not only of the king's power, but of God's. Under France's Old Regime, judicial torture was performed at Christian shrines. It was punctuated by Christian speeches: moralizing

---

[5] Rivera, "Glory: The First Passion of Theology?," 172.
[6] Ibid., 177.
[7] Michel Foucault, *Surveiller et punir: Naissance de la prison* (Paris: Gallimard, 1975), 9–11. I offer a fuller reading of these pages and the others cited here from Foucault in *Convulsing Bodies: Religion and Resistance in Foucault* (Stanford, CA: Stanford University Press, 2015).

admonitions, required confessions, cries for divine mercy. It was an earthly anticipation of eternal punishment—a theater of hell. So Foucault frequently describes it in religious terms, as a "rite" or "liturgy", a "ceremonial" and even a "festival".[8]

6. There is always another Execution, another Torture, in Christian writing. Writing bodily terror is one task for the author of a gospel—and so the task of many devotional writers who will study it. Meditations on Christ's passion have been for centuries a fixed genre of scriptural commentary.

After reading Isaiah's prophecy of the suffering servant, some Christian writers believed that Jesus was in fact ugly.[9] Most Christian writers on the Passion have stressed that Jesus was made ugly on the cross. Representations of the crucifixion vie in displaying his deformity—twisted limbs, gouges in bleeding skin, the appeal of agonized eyes.

I find the ugliness of Jesus's crucified body important so far as believers are asked to see it as an episode in the beauty of God. The crucifixion inverts ordinary bodily aesthetic by claiming that the radiant source of all beauty was once disclosed in a scourged and crucified body.[10] Julian of Norwich describes it graphically—too graphically for some readers. The head of Jesus, bleeding from its crown of thorns, is held over her during her own passion. She looks up at it: it is beautiful.[11] What is the difference between Julian writing her love for the crucified Jesus and the newspaper stories or eyewitness reports of the public torture of Damiens?

There is an account of the regicide's torture in the memoirs of Casanova, that connoisseur of sensations. He records it as a memorable spectacle—and offers as a proof of his own constancy that he was able to watch for most of four hours. At certain moments, he confesses, he had to close his eyes and cover his ears.[12]

What allows Julian to speak without indulging such salacious voyeurism? Julian suffers too, and so writes affliction as one of the afflicted. Imagine a record of the execution of Damiens soaked in the tears of his family. Imagine a literature of the terrible spectacles of blasphemous power written not for

---

[8] Foucault, *Surveiller et punir*, 14 ("la sombre fête punitive," "cérémonial de la peine"), 49 ("le théâtre de l'enfer"), 53 ("liturgie des supplices"), 54 ("rituel de la loi armée"), 61 ("de faire éclater rituellement sa réalité de surpouvoir"), and so on.

[9] See especially Isaiah 53:2–3. A useful introduction to this tradition can be found in Stephen D. Moore, *God's Beauty Parlor and Other Queer Spaces in and around the Bible* (Stanford, CA: Stanford University Press, 2001), 96–9.

[10] Compare Rivera, "Glory: The First Passion of Theology?," 175, on Dussel.

[11] Julian of Norwich, *Showings*, Edmund Colledge and James Walsh (eds), (Mahwah, NJ: Paulist Press, 1978), 128 ("everything around the cross was ugly to me"), 129 (blood), 136–7 (blood), 141 ("his freshness, his ruddiness, his vitality and his beauty" which, with death, now changes), and so on.

[12] Giacomo Casanova, *Mémoires de Jacques Casanova de Seingalt, écrits par lui-même* (Paris: Paulin, 1843), vol. 2, 377.

official archives, but for communities of the terrified.—That is one way of conceiving the genre of a gospel.

7. Imagine Christian theology as a literature of the crucified God soaked in the tears of Mary Magdalene—I mean, soaked in the tears of those who have gone looking for his missing body (John 20:11–18). This literature would expound the memories of Jesus's words and deeds. It would contemplate the repetition of the meal that he commanded. It might record unusual sightings or encounters, before and after his death. But on every page, it would mark an absence—even if it did predict a return.

Writing that paragraph, I seem to betray the rigorous history of theology into a species of sentimental literature. As if I had forgotten the distinction between dogma and devotion. As if I had ignored the warning signs posted along the borders separating theology from "mere literature."

Mourning Lost Beauties

8. Rivera writes under an epigraph from an essay by Virginia Woolf on the modern novel. She quotes Rubem Alves, José Saramago, and Eduardo Galeano, each writing back and forth across the boundary between theology or philosophy or criticism and literature.[13] Together with others in the 2011 *Polydoxy* collection, Rivera seems to find in literature a more apt or more beautiful rendering of the theology that she wants to write.

Not a few writers of "progressive theology" seem now to be haunted by a yearning for literature.[14] The yearning can be so strong on some pages—in some moments of my own writing—that I feel the impulse to interrupt: If you long for literature so much, why not write it? Why keep on writing only to mourn your choice of genre?

Counter-question: Is it clear that theology's mourning could now be ended—or that literary forms suited for it lie ready to hand?

9. Christian theology has always been haunted by the envy of a book it could not rival—I mean, the Christian Bible. The Bible was the standard of truth, but

---

[13] Rivera, "Glory: The First Passion of Theology?," 168 (Woolf and Alves), 169 (Saramago), 181 (Galeano). The epigraph from Woolf is taken from the essay, "Modern Fiction," originally published by the *TLS* in 1919 under the title "Modern Novels." It was revised for inclusion in *The Common Reader: The First Series*, from which Rivera quotes. I follow the version in Andrew McNeille (ed), *The Essays of Virginia Woolf*, vol. 4: *1925 to 1928* (London: The Hogarth Press, 1984), 157–65, here at 160–1.

[14] In *Polydoxy* itself, I note the extended, affectionate readings of Kay Ryan (by Schneider, "Crib Notes from Bethlehem," 21–9), of J. M. Coetzee (by Keller, "Be a Multiplicity: Ancestral Anticipations," 81–6), and of Octavia Butler (by Coleman, "Invoking Oya: Practicing a Polydox Soteriology through a Postmodern Womanist Reading of Tananarive Due's *The Living Blood*," 193–201).

also the rule of verbal beauty, especially when praising God. It was orthodox in both senses. The book of books, it compassed all honorable tropes and genres. It spoke in dozens of voices, each one appropriately shaped and abundant in effects.

In his *Confessions*, Augustine remembers how he was led slowly out of the arrogance of a youthful rhetor to appreciation for the lowly style of the Christian scriptures. At first, though young, he was not enough of a child to read the Bible.[15] His literary vanity prevented him from appreciating texts that affronted his so recently-acquired tastes. The scriptures appeared to Augustine "less worthy" than Cicero. They were less noble, but also less fantastical—too close to the earth and its vulnerable bodies.

Some decades later, when he comes to finish his book on Christian reading and writing, Augustine emphasizes not just the truth of the scriptures, but their unsurpassed rhetorical beauty. "For where I understand [the scriptural writers], not only can nothing seem to me wiser than they are, but nothing more eloquent."[16] He proceeds to lay out a double contrast between Christian scriptures and pagan rhetoric. "All those powers (*virtutes*) and ornaments of eloquence, about which they puff themselves up . . . [could be] shown in the sacred writings."[17] The scriptures contain all that is good in pagan rhetoric. "But it is not the things that these [scriptural] writers have in common with the Gentile orators and poets that give me more delight in their eloquence than I can say. I rather admire and wonder at the way in which, besides their own eloquence, they use our [civic] eloquence so that it is not conspicuous either by presence or absence." The scriptures can use Ciceronian rhetoric as an unaccented supplement because they already have a unique beauty of their own.

Christian theology yearns for the beauty of the biblical texts that are its origin, limit, and foundation. It comments on them or amplifies them, but it always ends by gesturing back towards them. Its highest beauties are quotations. So concludes Augustine, now grown up as a writer.

10. Modern Christian theology sometimes loses the scriptures in another way, by ceding them to the authority of philologists.

Applying the assumptions of historical criticism to the Christian Bible rectified many historical errors, but it also deprived theology of its oldest genres and its strongest styles. If serious scriptural commentary could now be written only by philologists, and if their objective commentaries proved

---

[15] Augustine, *Confessions*, 3.5.9, M. Skutella and L. Verheijen (eds), *Corpus Christianorum Series Latina*, vol. 27 (Turnhout: Brepols, 1981), 42.

[16] Augustine, *On Christian Teaching*, 4.6.9.25, R. P. H. Green (ed), Oxford Early Christian Studies (Oxford: Clarendon Press, 1995), 206.

[17] Augustine, *On Christian Teaching*, 4.6.10, p. 206, for this quotation and the one immediately following.

the scriptures a pedestrian patchwork, then theology had no warrant for efforts at writing.

Or theologians had to find warrant elsewhere. Rivera, following Woolf, retells scripture using a version of modernist narrative. In the essay that Rivera quotes, Woolf is talking about "the task of the novelist." Woolf's essay reviews narrative experiments in then recent novels, underlining their attempts to render the flow of embodied experience.

Rivera's experiment in scriptural retelling begins by inhabiting a scene. "I have imagined myself like Moses, wondering at the sight and warmth of the burning bush, barefoot, feeling the pebbles on the ground pressing against my feet."[18] The sentence is both an experiment and an echo. (Writers late in a tradition often experiment by unexpected retrieval or juxtaposition.) Perhaps she has in mind Kierkegaard's Johannes de Silentio and his (failed) retellings of Abraham in the dialectical lyric that is *Fear and Trembling*. Or perhaps she is recalling some older practices of Christian preaching and spiritual direction (say, the composition of place in the *Spiritual Exercises* of Ignatius of Loyola).

Woolf's description of the modern novelist's task gives Rivera warrant for retrieving old theological genres that once drew courage from scriptural forms. "Mere literature" supplies the impulse for resisting the erasure of scriptural eloquence as an (unattainable) ideal.

11. To draw one's courage for writing theology from the modern novel might seem to bind theology to the modern novel's nihilistic fate. Doesn't the modernist experiment end in exhaustion rather than praise? Woolf herself says that Joyce's experiments in *Ulysses* leave the readers "in a bright yet narrow room, confined and shut in, rather than enlarged and set free."[19]

Other readers of other modern novels thought that this suffocating room was God's mausoleum.

The Terror of Silence

12. In the 1960s, a decade that began for him with a quickly famous book on madness, Foucault wrote texts that are typically grouped together as "literary." These texts retell a long pursuit of the holy or the divine beyond the edge of efficient reason—in the empty space left by the flight of God or gods. The last possibility had been hinted at throughout Foucault's *History of Madness* whenever he returned to an implied canon of writers or artists whose efforts—at madness, at creation—placed them outside managed language or thought. The canon typically includes Hölderlin, Nerval, Van Gogh,

---

[18] Rivera, "Glory: The First Passion of Theology?," 177.
[19] Woolf, "Modern Fiction," 162.

Nietzsche, and Artaud.[20] Foucault associates them with the collapse of speech, but also with forgotten ceremonies, acts of blasphemy, and unnerving apostleship.

In the 1960s, Foucault did not write directly about this canon. He writes instead about three writers whom he regularly names together: Georges Bataille, Pierre Klossowski, and Maurice Blanchot. Reading these three, explicating them, he negotiates an inheritance of the canon of a divine madness that shatters—or completes—language.

13.   Towards the end of this so-called "literary period," Foucault agreed to be interviewed by Claude Bonnefoy in the hopes of producing a book of conversations. The book never appeared. Foucault broke off with the claim that he was uncomfortable talking about his own practice of writing.[21] One can sympathize: Bonnefoy's questions often push towards the sort of biographical explanation of his authorship that Foucault famously resisted for all authorship. The transcription of the interviews that did take place shows Foucault trying on different accounts of what attracts him to writing—including the writing of his "mad" canon.

Foucault explains that he is not interested in a more exact diagnosis of the authors whose madness figures so prominently in their fame. He is not even interested in the relation of authorial biography to text. He is interested rather in how it is that speech labeled as mad comes to be so immediately influential in the literature of those designated as sane.[22] The officially unintelligible murmurings of the mad—confined by Reason to the asylum—suddenly appear on this side of the walls as literature. As if the unspeakable were now spoken, but only on condition of becoming literature.

14.   Talking to Bonnefoy, Foucault claims not to be fascinated "personally" by the "sacred side of writing." He acknowledges that a series of European writers, including at least one from his alternate canon, have shown that writing "has a sacred dimension, that it is a sort of activity in itself, not transitive."[23]

Earlier, Foucault had written an admiring, imitative essay to Blanchot's notion of the experience of "the outside (*dehors*)." The experience appeared for European readers in Sade's monologue of naked desire.[24] Foucault links it next

---

[20] For example, Michel Foucault, *Folie et déraison: Histoire de la folie à l'âge classique* (Paris: Plon, 1961), 35, 299, 416–7, 424–6, 439, 456, 612, 636, 641–3.

[21] The interviews were conducted most probably in the summer and fall of 1968. See the framing remarks by Philippe Artières in Michel Foucault, *Le beau danger: Entretien avec Claude Bonnefoy* (Paris: Éditions EHESS, 2011), 19, 24.

[22] Ibid., 53.

[23] Ibid., 28.

[24] Foucault, "La pensée du dehors," in *Dits et écrits*, Daniel Defert and François Ewald (eds), (Paris: NRF / Gallimard, 1994), vol. 1, 521–3, for this and the rest of the "canon".

to Hölderlin's manifestation of the "scintillating absence of the gods," under-stood as a new obligation to attend to the endless consequences of " 'God's failure.' " Together Sade and Hölderlin leave behind, for their successors, for some "us", these floating reminders of the impossibility of a stable "I".

It is Blanchot who gathers the reminders as critic and as novelist. Blanchot is "for us this very thought itself—the real presence, absolutely distant, scintillating, invisible, the necessary fate, the inevitable law, the calm, infinite, measured vigor of this thought itself." The absent God has become the absent author—and Blanchot is not so much its prophet as its sacrament, its "real presence." Reading Blanchot well, we seem to receive the communion of authorial language, we almost consume the thought of outside.[25]

Except that we do not. Foucault insists with Blanchot that there neither is nor can be such communion. Blanchot's novels and essays may look like the negative theology of Christian tradition—may seem somehow to resemble the famous texts of the Dionysian corpus. But if negative theology requires passing "outside of oneself", it does so only in order to find the self again at the end, wrapped in the "dazzling interiority of a word that is fully Being and Word."[26] How different Blanchot is from (Christian) mysticism, which always ends by recuperating any temporally lost self in the presence of the communicating Word![27]

When the modern novel reaches its appointed end, there is nothing higher, nothing hidden, no goal or secret. There is only the space "outside"—the emptiness around language, of language.

15. Foucault recalls these teachings. He also associates his writing with a part of them. A justification of writing as re-actualization of a "living word that is at once the word of human beings and—probably—of God, this is profoundly foreign to me. For me, writing begins after death and once this rupture is established. Writing is for me the drift of after-death and not the pursuit of the source of life. It is perhaps in this that the form of my language is profoundly anti-Christian, and [the form] is doubtless more so than the themes that I do not cease to treat."[28] There is no possibility of resurrection through writing, much less any persuasive hope for it.

16. Foucault sometimes endorses this view of language as the culmination of his engagement with recent literature. A reader might then imagine that

---

[25] In an essay on Flaubert's *St. Anthony*, Foucault describes the book as the first "literary work that has its proper place only in the space of books" (*Dits et écrits*, vol. 1, 298). Others that follow in this canon are Mallarmé, Joyce, Roussel, Kafka, Pound, and Borges—but not (yet) Blanchot.

[26] Foucault, "La pensée du dehors," 521.

[27] Ibid., 537. Foucault had insisted earlier that Pierre Klossowski's engagement with Christian apophatic motifs ought not to be confused with negative theology itself. See Foucault, "La prose d'Actéon," in *Dits et écrits*, vol. 1, 334.

[28] Foucault, *Le beau danger*, 39.

Foucault's next step would be either to stop writing altogether or to write novels in the manner of Blanchot. In fact, Foucault does neither. He goes on to write about bodies and powers.

Foucault tells Bonnefoy that his own experience of writing is rather different from both the canon of the mad and the modern novels that inspired Blanchot. Foucault came to appreciate writing after finding himself blocked from expression—by the struggle to master legible handwriting, by the experience of trying to speak while teaching abroad. The blockage led him to recognize in his own language a familiar "physiognomy," a habitable topography. He began to want to write just to "build a little house of language of which I would be the master while knowing all the corners."[29]

Later in the interview, Foucault describes his sense of the enigma or paradox in daily writing. "How is it that the act—so fictive, narcissistic, folded over itself—of sitting down at the desk in the morning and then covering a certain number of blank pages can have the effect of a blessing (*bénédiction*) on the rest of the day? How can the reality of things ... be transfigured just because this [writing] has happened in the morning, or because one can do it during the day?"[30]

No resurrection in Foucault's writing (he declares), yet both benediction and transfiguration (he admits with puzzlement).

17. At the very beginning of his interview with Bonnefoy, Foucault confesses some apprehension. He doesn't know how he will be able to speak. "Perhaps because I am an academic, I have a certain number of forms of speech that are in some way statutory. There are the things that I write, which are intended for composing articles, books—in other words, discursive and explanatory texts."[31] But to speak in an interview about his writing is to speak outside the statutory forms.

Foucault must be teasing. Every one of his long texts and many of the shorter ones have already broken the academic rules. By the time of the interview with Bonnefoy, he has already navigated various versions of the interview. So if he is anxious about breaking the rules, they must be his own rules against self-disclosure. (He would enforce those rules against himself when he abandoned the project with Bonnefoy.) Or else Foucault's anxiety is the deeper fear of writing or speaking in startling, unknown forms. As if one were mad.

18. The editors of *Polydoxy* begin by drawing our attention to the survival of theological writing, which continues after so many proclamations of its

---

[29] Ibid., 31.
[30] Ibid., 56.
[31] Ibid., 26.

demise.[32] They suggest that theology survives in part by multiplying sources, and they then turn to "multiplicity itself" as a new source for their own writing.

I share in the hope for a rebirth of theological language outside the atrophying institutions to which it has been confined, but I worry that we don't understand well enough the reasons internal to theology for its present weakness. It isn't just that opponents wished for the demise of our seminaries or that economic disruptions suddenly cut off the funding for them. Within theology itself, and especially within its language, there have long been signs of necrosis.

To say this differently: much theology still gets written in dead forms, without any credible promise of transfiguration or benediction, much less of resurrection. Indeed, with the internet as vanity press, there may now be more public speech about theology, amateur and professional, than ever before. Not much of it shows signs of life.

19. In the essay from which Rivera quotes, Woolf professes a sort of astonishment that so many novels are being written when they seem to lack their essential ingredient—namely, the representation of life. Woolf's remarks about life are part of an exhortation to find new forms for the novel. One form is adumbrated in Joyce, perhaps, though she concludes that its fulfillment lies beyond *Ulysses*, in the space between the English novel and the Russian. Woolf sets the Russian novelists apart, as the masters not only of modern form, but of the narration of spiritual life.

There is some silliness in Woolf about national characters, but there is also a compelling call for authorial courage. "The problem before the novelist at present, as we suppose it to have been in the past, is to contrive means of being free to set down what he [*sic*] chooses. He has to have the courage to say that what interests him is no longer 'this' but 'that': out of 'that' alone must he construct his work."[33]

20. A theological writer—late in a tradition that has professed but never learned the humility of apophasis, surrounded by mechanically reproduced "orthodoxy"—must still find the courage to say that what lures her writing is not this, but that. That unrecognized body of the dead rabbi. That bent beauty.

The Politics of Apophasis

21. Jesus was tortured and then executed by the local agents of an endlessly loquacious imperial power that failed to make note of him until after he was

---

[32] Keller and Schneider, "Introduction," *Polydoxy*, 1.
[33] Woolf, "Modern Fiction," 162.

long gone. There were more important items to record in its archives—and other orthodoxies to enforce.

Christians learned to speak in the interstices of empire. They appear in some early texts as stubborn fanatics who violate all the rules of civil speech. Soon enough they are using the imperial mechanisms to amplify their speech and then impose it.

22. We write theology—when we do—much later in the Christian tradition, after the collapse of many Christendoms, but still hedged about by them. Finding the courage to write theology requires not only the choice to follow divine lures, but the brave conviction that imperial brutalities have not yet corrupted the Christian language used to bless them.

23. Rivera writes: "A counterfeit of glory has lodged itself in the infamous trinity of God, gold, and glory, which is commonly used as shorthand for the motives of the Spanish conquest of America."[34] It is only one of many counterfeits in the succession of Christendoms. But the Spanish conquest—so ambitious, so grandly documented, so enduring—brings into sharp focus the precarious situation of theological speech. Christian theology was imported to the Spanish colonies with the force of arms. That is terrifying enough. But the Spanish conquerors rapidly replicated all the structures for producing theological speech. There were universities and seminaries, schools for translators and iconographers. The extraordinary campaign of religious building divided up the landscape with a network of sanctuaries, but also libraries and archives. Theology arrived not just as a cargo, but as an industry.

A counterfeit glory, yes, but one wrapped around practices of theological writing that we inherit—and not only from what we still call Latin America.

24. What does it mean to write theology after colonization has been inscribed into our speech? We may want to dismiss all colonizers' theology as corruption, but then we would have almost nothing left—and no body from which to speak, since our bodies, all of them, have been hybridized by histories of conquest.

There are no racially pure bodies. Neither are there pure languages, whether for tribes or individuals. The English I learned as an infant was a polyglot pastiche. I heard it alongside Mediterranean French and Mexican Spanish. My "mother tongue" was spoken to me in loving instruction, but also as anger or deceit. Its praise was often used to control. We receive all languages by a kind of colonization, but they are the only languages we have for writing about God.

---

[34] Rivera, "Glory: The First Passion of Theology?," 170.

We look in colonizing theology for the inevitable slips of encounter, for the unavoidable flickering of self-awareness.

25. "Images of a lost (but still real) earthly paradise" were written over the colonial landscape in violent disregard of its all too real populations.[35] But the utopian seed, the lure of an alternate community or another history, also inspired passionate returns to the idea of original Christian fellowship—and powerful imaginings of reborn Christian speech. With the conversion of indigenous civilizations, whole libraries of early Christianity seemed to come alive: the saintly sagas of preaching to unbaptized cities of glittering wealth.

Retrieving an old theological form means reactivating it as a lure—as exhortation or manuduction. Spanish missionaries read patristic tales of pagan encounter as instructions for how to persuade.

26. How is theology possible in a "decolonial" condition?[36] If the work of de-colonization is hardly finished in former colonies, it is equally unfinished in former empires—or present ones.

How does theology recover from its own imperial adventures? It should begin by abjuring them, of course. It can then attempt to learn all the lessons it once refused to hear from those it tried to subjugate. But it must confess that imperial impulses have not disappeared—and that they are not confined only to some nations or peoples. The work of decolonizing theology can never be finished until the final disappearance of what theology calls "sin." It is not within human power to ensure that disappearance.

Decolonial theology is the theology of those who speak some truth about the terror of colonization. This includes the truth that colonization is always ready to begin again—even among those who have suffered it.

27. Decolonizing theology means imagining anti-imperial characters and communities without succumbing to the fantasy that finding the right words will magically embody them. Empires too like incantations.

I begin, in any case, by rewriting myself—by making new speech, which is not always the same as making new words. I can make it by acknowledging the bombastic emptiness of the subject that has been speaking or that even now speaks. Certainly I rewrite myself by inhabiting the stories of a community of speech yet to come. Only this speech must arrive without conquest.

28. In a preface to a collection of documents, Foucault sketches the range of feelings he has experienced when coming across written traces of actual lives

---

[35] Ibid.
[36] Ibid., 183, note 21, on the meaning of "decolonial."

in the official archives: "an emotion, laughter, surprise, a certain fright or some other feeling, of which I would perhaps find it difficult to justify the intensity now that the first moment of discovery has passed."[37] Foucault calls these laconic biographies "strange poems" or "poem-lives."[38] But he also insists that his first encounter with them "agitated more fibers in me that what one ordinarily calls literature." In these records of a growing state power, Foucault sees among other things "the beauty of this classical style draped in a few sentences over persons who were doubtless miserable."[39]

If Foucault is fascinated by the growing use of chancery style to record not only great crimes but domestic miseries, he also notices how those miseries expose the pretentions of power. Beyond what literature could accomplish, the criminal registers or royal petitions show how ordinary bodies must "dress up in tatters of fabric ... if they want to be noticed on the scene of power ... a poor troupe of buffoons, who would deck themselves out however they could in a few flashy rags (*oripeaux*) that were once sumptuous."[40]

Some two years later, reflecting on the stagecraft of a late Roman emperor, Foucault will turn the same image into a more general question about all power: "Can there be a power without its flashy rags?"[41]

Foucault sometimes wants to efface himself before the archives of human misery by adhering to a strict art of quotation, but he cannot stop himself from writing out his reactions to the drag of power—to desperate imitations of it, but also to the spectacle that power must make of itself.

Readers as Speakers

29. If I began by asking, Who is glorified in polydoxy?, and then asked, Who writes or speaks or performs the glorification?, I have still to pose a third question, perhaps the most important: For whom—for which audience?

Woolf has said that the courage to write supposes freedom, and she has pictured it as solitary. Her picture is incomplete. A writer's solitude requires a whole host of favorable circumstances—as she would argue at length in *A Room of One's Own*. Those circumstances include a community of readers, especially readers who are fellow writers.

---

[37] Foucault, "La vie des hommes infâmes," in *Dits et écrits*, vol. 3, 237.
[38] Ibid., 237, 239.
[39] Ibid., 238
[40] Ibid., 250.
[41] Foucault, *Du gouvernement des vivants: Cours au Collège de France, 1979–1980*, Michel Senellart (ed), François Ewald and Alessandro Fontana (dirs), (Paris: EHESS, Gallimard, and Seuil, 2012), 18.

30. If retrieving or discovering a form of theological writing means activating it as a lure, then every form foreshadows a community of response—a community of readers with the capacities or characters for responding to that lure.

31. So much church reading is compelled. In liturgical churches, prayers, scriptures, and even sermons are "appointed to be read." In churches that reject liturgy, there are still scriptures, the required reading of which is further controlled by obligatory commentary or interpretation. Church-goers turn to theology most often under compulsion.

Conditions are not so different in "the academy." Sometimes we professors read for unmixed pleasure or out of curiosity. More often, we read something because we have to do so. It is on a reading list. It issues from a powerful authority. It is the latest fad. It must be reviewed or graded.

Perhaps for these reasons, little academic theology gives evidence of wanting to attract or create an audience—however much it declares that it wants to change the world. Readers are presumed to exist, and some hierarchy will guarantee their attention.

I want to say: The arduous purpose of theological writing is luring readers into forms of speech that none of you has been taught to read, much less to speak.

32. What is the genre of the book, *Polydoxy*? At one point, the editors write that the volume entertains a "doctrinal claim" about what it means to be Christian in this world.[42] Of course, it is not a doctrinal work in any standard sense.

The anthology reads more like a manifesto. I concede at once that "manifesto" has had many meanings over the last two centuries. Texts claiming that title have been written in various forms for all sorts of purposes. Still *Polydoxy* is a manifesto in the sense that it combines declaration and exhortation to propose a new kind of theology that would have many effects, at once conceptual, psychological, and social.

How does *Polydoxy* hope to endow its title word with the power to change theological language? How will it make its neologism a new coinage rather than a nonce term? The anthology spins discourses around the word. Some link it to a textual past. Others show how it might move in rewritten stories. Still others promise—or fantasize—that adopting the new word will undo at least some of the disastrous consequences of mono-orthodoxy.

33. We come at the end of a century and a half littered with manifestos. A few, like Marx's *Communist Manifesto*, are supposed to have had enduring

---

[42] Keller and Schneider, "Introduction," *Polydoxy*, 4.

effects—though it is never clear to me whether these texts were much more than convenient emblems for movements that succeeded by less verbal means. Other manifestos, like Breton's first *Surrealist Manifesto*, enjoyed some fame, but then faded—or required corrective sequels. Most manifestos are now read by historians not as active appeals, but as inert evidence for some story the texts didn't mean to tell.

34. What would it be for *Polydoxy* to succeed as a manifesto? Would it lead to curricular reforms, international congresses, denominational resolutions—in short, to the imposition of a new orthodoxy? Then it would betray itself.

Its success must rather be the slow spread of a practice of writing through interstitial communities. The practice would not multiply commentaries on *Polydoxy*, nor would it simply imitate it. Much less would it elevate it into a scripture never to be rivaled.

35. In its own writing, in its example of communal production, *Polydoxy* encourages its readers to overcome the terrors of writing theology—the imperial terrors that theology can authorize, but perhaps even more the solitary terrors of a blank page not yet written in a language that no one now is quite able to speak.

Virginia Woolf was right to speak of the need for courage. Courage, the first passion of theological writing.

Modern Theology 30:3 July 2014
ISSN 0266-7177 (Print)
ISSN 1468-0025 (Online)

DOI: 10.1111/moth.12124

"THERE IS HOPE FOR A TREE": LAMENT AND HOPE IN CONVERSATION WITH POLYDOXY

WENDY FARLEY

For there is hope for a tree,
If it be cut down, that it will sprout again,
And that its shoots will not cease.
Though its root grow old in the earth,
And its stump die in the ground,
Yet at the scent of water it will bud
And put forth branches like a young plant.

Job 14:7–9

I look over a thrice clear-cut forest, its mosses, its angular firs and pines perhaps only scraps of a former loveliness. Its sheer existence is a poignant insistence not only to live, but to be beautiful. My eyes wander over the Sound and my heart leaps at the shimmer of light and darkness of moving waves. But it breaks in the knowledge that these teaming, life-filled oceans are dying.[1] According to the Climate Project, "Nine of the ten hottest years on record were in the past twelve years. Just in recent months, extreme rainfall and floods have affected us everywhere from the Mississippi Valley to Beijing. Superstorm Sandy both devastated human lives and led to tens of billions of dollars in damages. The most severe drought in decades spread over half the United States. Climate change is already happening, and it

Wendy Farley
Department of Religion, Emory University, 537 Kilgo Circle, Callaway S214, Atlanta, GA 30322, USA
Email: mfarley@emory.edu
    [1] http://www.bbc.co.uk/news/science-environment-13796479; see also http://theclimate project.org/news/article/463.

has entered our daily lives."[2] What litany of statistics might awaken a deluded population to the slow death to which our planet is being subjected? What piercing anecdote of an animal's—or species'—demise might finally wound hearts indifferent to the suffering and destruction being wrought? What calculation of self-interest or compassion for humanity might discern in storms, wild-fires, droughts, floods, starvation and thirst a crisis that begs for redress?[3]

As evening approaches, how will we live with the mass death that has been the effect of our "axial age:" cultural genocide, physical genocide, endless war, slavery, the misery of socially-constructed poverty, the misery of women reduced to sexual slavery within or outside of marriage? If we were to recognize the horror of this violence, would we better prepared to recognize the fast approaching limit of the Earth's capacity to tolerate our predations? Acknowledging our history of anti-Semitism, slavery and Jim Crow we seem (partly) to awaken from a dream. What once seemed obvious and normal seem now to be appalling symbols of human evil. We are puzzled, self-righteous, outraged that Germans so utterly failed to resist Hitler's orgy of death, that they so glibly sacrificed almost every vestige of rationality. What will people in the next generation or two think of us?

Scientists are observing and anticipating the largest loss of species in the earth's history in the coming years, a loss that is coming more quickly than earlier models predicted.[4] Food insecurity affected a billion people in 2010 and is understood to become worse as a result of hotter and more violent weather.[5] The UN Environmental Program reported in 2000 full-scale

---

[2] Climate Reality Project; http://climaterealityproject.org/the-climate-crisis/ (April, 2013).

[3] Summaries of the extent and intensity of the environmental crisis we now face can be found in many places. One good place to start is Al Gore's recent article in the *Rolling Stone*: http://www.rollingstone.com/politics/news/climate-of-denial-20110622. Other organizations that have websites and articles include the Alliance for Climate Protection (2006 Nobel Laureate), InterAcademy Council, European Academy of Sciences and Arts, UN Environmental Program, Center for New American Security, NASA, and the Intergovernmental Panel on Climate Change. The NAACP also has a section on the effects of climate change on people of color. BBC News usually runs articles about the environment and climate change several times a week on its website. By contrast, news media in the US are almost completely silent.

[4] "Many scientists today believe that Earth is on the verge of the most significant mass extinction of plant and animal life in 65 million years, perhaps in the entire history of the planet, and certainly in the history of human life on the planet. Human societies around the world depend on access to diverse species—a condition called 'biodiversity'—in ways that are obvious, and not so obvious. Biodiversity loss is likely to be highly destabilizing, in that it will constrain access to a full range of natural resources, including food and potable water" (Center for New American Security, http://www.cbd.int/). This point is echoed by Wendell Berry, who reminds us that 25 billion tons of topsoil are lost each year, that the most abundant species of marine life have become commercially extinct and that when we also consider things like the use of river systems for waste disposal, air pollution, and radioactive waste, we might recognize that these planetary disturbances place us at the "terminal phase of the Cenozoic Era"; Berry, *The Great Work: Our Way into the Future* (New York: Broadway Books, 2000), 3–4.

[5] http://theclimateproject.org/news/article/462. The Center for New American Security identifies environmental issues as crucial to national security: "In the 21st century, the security of

emergencies, including severe water shortage, loss of topsoil, irreversible destruction of rain forest and biodiversity. They cited poverty in most of the world and excessive consumption as primary causes of environmental degradation and called for a 90% reduction of natural resource usage by the developed world.[6] The death tolls of Katrina and the current famine in the horn of Africa, the heat-related deaths of human beings, livestock, flora and fauna appear to be harbingers of much more devastating suffering and death to come.[7]

"The owl of Minerva flies at dusk." As Christians for whom universal love translates into justice and activism, it is right to struggle against systems that deceive and destroy. But as theologians it is also right to pause and ponder. Understanding, a thing for the gods (*Phaedrus*), may elude us, but simply to meditate on this moment of history may be useful. To find ways to tolerate, in however small doses, the truth of loss, may open to a counter-narrative in which beauty and life still sparkle with grace. Perhaps "counter-narrative" is still too cognitive. Meditation may open on a "feeling" (as Schleiermacher or Whitehead might put it) of holy presence in this mangled moment.

One opening for such meditation is the work of the authors collecting themselves under the term "polydoxy." These writers identify thought patterns in Christianity and in our common, western, modern culture that have proven toxic. They find resources in literature, religious dialogue, forgotten writers, and ignored experiences to refresh our understanding of Christian narratives and symbols. This movement is associated with a particular cast of characters and reflects a style of language and, for many authors, an appreciation of the contributions of post-modern philosophy to contemporary theology. These idioms will not be adopted by or even appreciated by all readers. But the themes and issues they raise are urgently important. It will be useful to recognize common ground between these writers and others who are concerned about similar issues: who are troubled by the ways in which the church can be harmful, authoritarian, or idolatrous; who are

---

nations will depend increasingly on the security of natural resources, or 'natural security.' Beginning in 2009, CNAS analysts began collaborating with a consortium of environmental groups and members of the security community to explore in-depth the real role natural resources play in a variety of U.S. national security and foreign policy concerns. Countries around the world rely on the availability of potable water, arable land, fish stocks, biodiversity, energy, minerals and other renewable and non-renewable resources to meet the rising needs and expectations of a growing world population. Yet the availability of these resources is by no means assured"; http://www.cnas.org/naturalsecurity/consequences/biodiversity. By way of example, they point out that in Afghanistan, which derives 50% of its GDP from agriculture and ranching, frequent droughts in combination with unsustainable land use and deforestation have put 75% of land area at risk of desertification. Water scarcity and pollution reduce Pakistan's irrigation capabilities and agricultural productivity. Yemen is at risk of complete environmental collapse as both its water and oil reserves decline. The loss of Mexico's forests and fisheries has long influenced economic stability and internal security dynamics.

[6] http://news.bbc.co.uk/2/hi/science/nature/447767.stm
[7] http://theclimateproject.org/news/article/475.

called to respond to injustice and suffering whether their emphasis is in the direction of challenging "lock-down America," the environmental crisis, human oppression, traumatic suffering, or comforting the sick or dying; who seek to expand the resources of Christian theology to include less familiar texts, methods and dialogue partners; who—as devoted lovers or battered wives of the church—adore the Good in any of its forms. By engaging their work, perhaps we will each in our way participate in possibilities for novelty, adventure, zest, and peace.

Totalities and Totalitarianisms: The Logic of the One

Polydox authors challenge the idea of orthodoxy in the sense of a single, uniform, authoritative, more or less unchanging, utterly reliable and certain belief structure, complete with a disciplinary apparatus to uphold it. There are many reasonable and good possible meanings of orthodoxy. One of my colleagues pointed out the importance of some distinction between orthodoxy and heresy to condemn forms of Christianity that integrated apartheid or torture into its beliefs and practices. Its appreciation of multiplicity and ambiguity may make polydoxy open to such an interpretation. But granting the usefulness of some meanings of orthodoxy, it remains crucial—as a Christian spiritual practice—to acknowledge the original sin or wound of the "logic of the one" that poisons much of the Christian tradition.

Schneider and Keller point out the dual impulses within Christianity to sustain a great variety of voices and lineages as well as a "habit of producing heretics as outer boundary markers for orthodox identity [which] exposes a repressive evasion of evident Christian complexity."[8] They propose an alternative to "Procrustean practices that chop off whole limbs of experience to fit a dominant theological frame of oneness" (Schneider and Keller, "Introduction," 3).[9]

The tension in the tradition between including many perspectives and condemning opponents as heretical goes back to the New Testament itself. In addition to the plurality of gospels and impulses toward universal salvation, there is an often-repeated anxiety over "false" versions of the Christian message. 2 Peter, 3 John, and Jude identify an opponent only on the basis of his message's being false. We do not know what we should believe, or even what the debate was about. But we are inducted into a world in which wrong

---

[8] "Introduction," Catherine Keller and Laurel C. Schneider, (ed) *Polydoxy: Theology of Multiplicity and Relation* (New York: Routledge, 2010), 2. Subsequent references to *Polydoxy* will be cited internally with author, essay title and page number.

[9] Laurel Schneider develops this description and critique of the logic of the One in much more detail in *Beyond Monotheism* (New York: Routledge, 2008). Much of Catherine Keller's work, in particular *The Face of the Deep: a Theology of Becoming* (New York: Routledge, 2003) also develops both a critique and a sustained alternative theology to this unitary habit of mind. Though John Thatamanil rejects the idea of multiple ultimates as incoherent (Thatamanil, "God as ground, contingency, and relation," 243), he recounts a sense of divine multiplicity inherent in the Trinity with great philosophical sophistication.

belief has ultimate consequences and fellow-traveling Christians may be demonically inspired. The writers defending the true faith were usually inventing this faith as they went, often breaking with previous interpretations to do so. Paul's inclusion of Gentiles, for which we Gentiles might be grateful, was nonetheless quite an innovation. John's high Christology, as beautiful as it is, was a huge leap beyond earlier writings. In point of fact, the New Testament is rife with multiple points of view: different models for understanding incarnation, eschatology, salvation, the timing of the crucifixion, the names of the "Twelve," economic justice, the role of women or slaves, the Trinity (if such a doctrine can be found in the New Testament at all), and the relationship of the Father to the Son. Paul and James represent opposite views of the relative merits of faith and works. The works united under John's name relentlessly insist that it is love that unites us with the divine but it is easy to find other texts that emphasize avoiding the dangers of impure living as the key to eternal life. The inexhaustible goodness of the divine not only permits but requires this multi-dimensional refraction. "Wherever we are on our journey" we will find something appropriate to our understanding and capacity. Buddhists call this *upaya*: skillful means. The Holy One appears to us in a way that we can tolerate, a physician with remedies for every kind of wound and disease. A trickster, the Incarnate One takes on the form necessary for each person's, each community's, each epoch's transformation.[10] The New Testament writings are soaked in the news that the Holy One is outrageously loving, bringing us new shoes, rings, a fatted calf when, strictly speaking, we do not deserve even to work as a hired hand. The condemnation of the practice of judging others runs through the gospels and the letters from Paul. And still this anxiety that if we do not get it "right" we are doomed is built into these very testimonies.

There are many dangers inherent in trying to turn the rich and diverse—even contradictory—wisdom of scripture into a single, authoritative creed. Any single thread pulled out occludes those threads that stand in tension with it. Assent to a doctrine or belief is an astonishingly thin spiritual practice. Even if the belief were "true" it would satisfy only the thinnest level of our being. Such dependence on cognitive acts belies the apophatic depths of personhood, cutting off these depths from the transforming power of the gospel. But how can any of our words about the divine be literally or adequately "true?" Our words are wooden idols; Isaiah is eloquent about the futility of worshiping anything less than God as divine.

But the history of Christianity has been only too robust in manifesting the corrupting and violent effects of conflating power and unilateral truth. As

---

[10] Sara McClintock's article on the Buddha as a trickster has fascinating resonance with a Christian interpretation of Jesus: "Compassionate Trickster: the Buddha as literary Character in the Narratives of Early Indian Buddhism," *Journal of the American Academy of Religion*, Vol. 79, no. 1 (March 2011), 90–112.

Rome roiled and eventually fell, the bishops of the church deified and mimicked the kind of authority represented by Caesar. Rejecting the pluralism that vivifies faith, they took up the very instruments of terror that had so traumatized generations of pre-Constantinian Christians. Forgetting that love unites us to the divine, they demanded assent to doctrine. Unmindful of the condemnations of strife and conflict as works of the flesh, they sought a false unity that excluded sometimes as much as half of Christian practitioners.[11] The thirteenth century saw great refinements in the instruments of coercion as policing of belief, sexuality, economic ideals by stake, torture, and harsh penitential practices transformed institutional Christianity into a totalitarian enterprise. Wars and repression followed until a weary world turned to science and secularism to defuse the relentless violence of religion. This legacy of religious totalitarianisms and violence helped create a public space emptied of living ethical ideals.[12] We are left with an interpretation of healing that is tyrannized by the objectifications of science, and a suspicion of "spirituality" as a New Age irrelevance. Christianity finds it difficult to bring balm to the deep places of the human spirit in part because its insistence on "orthodox" teaching cedes intellectual openness, healing, and spiritual practice to other experts. If young people flee the church because its exclusionary rhetoric makes no moral sense and the emptiness of belief proves too thin, is not Christianity itself to blame for having preferred "right" teaching to unconditional divine love?[13]

If we are uncomfortable, even dissident, about the effects of orthodoxy, we still are shaped by the logic of the One. By accepting this narrative of church history, we tacitly accept the claim that there is nothing outside the totality, there is nothing but orthodoxy: except, of course, heresy. But heresy is not Christianity. Marguerite Porete was, by definition, a heretic because she was condemned by church authorities. She who, like martyrs of old, held fast to a vision of the enormous love of the divine for the world; who practiced this love for herself and others; who moved into the depths of the divine unknowing and remembered the limitations of words, authorities, institutions; who, like the women apostles whose folly the disciples rejected, accepted her role as a teacher. Though they deployed steel and fire to destroy her, the authorities that condemned her were the true, orthodox Christians. It is difficult to conceive of Porete as the legitimate heir of Priscilla and Felicity.

---

[11] See Elaine Pagels, *Beyond Belief: the Secret Gospel of Thomas* (New York: Random House, 2003), 174. This description of the rise of unilateral orthodoxy is developed in greater detail in the first chapter of my work, *Gathering Those Driven Away: A Theology of Incarnation* (Louisville, KY: Westminster John Knox Press, 2011).

[12] Sharon Betcher ("Take my yoga upon you: a spiritual pli for the global city," 57–80) and Brianne Donaldson (" 'They'll know we are process thinkers by our . . .': finding the ecological ethics of Whitehead through the lens of Jainism and ecofeminist care," 203–216) provide examples of polydoxy's struggle for ethical ideals and disciplines.

[13] See, for example, Laurel Schneider's eloquent defense of love in the context of multiplicity in the concluding pages of *Beyond Monotheism*, especially 202–7.

We are trained, even if we dislike their techniques, to accept that "the church" is authoritative, orthodox, lineal descendants of the disciples. The church's "other" must, by definition be wrong, heretical. This habit of mind is difficult to reshape. But it leaves us in an unpleasant bind. We must accept the grand narrative as we receive it from church historians and theologians or, finding this narrative unbearable and at least partly untrue, we must leave. There is nothing exterior to totalitarianism. There is no "other." We fall into the void.

Putting it like this reflects the other side of the seductions of the "logic of the One." It imagines that Christianity is one thing and, in the spirit of Calvin, sees it all as poisoned, as Babylon's whore. But, as the polydox thinkers insist, the reduction of plurality to any one has never been successful. It is the great power of the logic of the One to so insist that there is only one that we come to believe it. But this is the great deception perpetrated by totalizing, totalitarian logic. The logic of the One would obscure from us the good company we find outside the totality: all the other religions, contemplative practices, heterodox lovers of Christ (Origen, John Scotus Erigena, Porete, Hus, Huguenots, Recusants, Shakers, Quakers, feminists, queers—a beatific cloud of witnesses). Discouraged dissenters may also operate out of the binary of an oppressive orthodox totality and its heretical others when we fail to recognize the ordinary, life-giving nurture that occurs in small and large congregations of every denomination or trivialize the good work done by denominational institutions to alleviate suffering and struggle toward more inclusive embodiments. Purging our own habit of totalizing thought, we become more attentive to the glories of multiplicity represented in the church's imperfections as well as in the great variety of its healthy expressions. Attending to the ordinary goodness of the church contributes its own discipline toward breaking free of the binary that can obscure the multiplicity of witnesses to Christian faith.[14]

Learned Ignorance

The intellectual source that waters this discipline of critique and celebration is sustained attention to the apophatic depths of the divine life. Textually, this

---

[14] Monica Coleman ("Invoking oya : practicing a polydox soteriology through a postmodern womanist reading of Tananarive Due's *The living blood*," 186–202) re-envisions salvation by attending to womanist science fiction and the Yoruba orisha; John Thatamanil ("God as ground, contingency, and relation: trinitarian polydoxy and religious diversity," 238–257) reconstructs Trinitarian theology in conversation with Hinduism and Buddhism; Hyo-Dong Lee (" 'Empty and tranquil, and without any sign, and yet all things are already luxuriantly present': a comparative theological reflection on the manifold Spirit," 126–150) reflects on a doctrine of Spirit with the help of neo-Confucianism; Marion Grau ("Signs taken for polydoxy in a Zulu Kraal: creative friction manifested in missionary-native discourse," 217–237) alerts us to the importance of a Zulu worldview; and Brianne Donaldson (" 'They'll know we are process thinkers by our . . .': finding the ecological ethics of Whitehead through the lens of Jainism and ecofeminist care," 203–216) deepens an ecological ethic in dialogue with Jainism.

means recovering resources in the tradition that fall outside the broad river of Augustine, Aquinas, Luther, Calvin, Barth, von Balthasar, Rahner, Tillich. Gems of Christian wisdom become again part of our understanding of the breadth and scope of tradition: Pseudo-Dionysius, Evagrius Ponticus, Maximus, Marguerite Porete, Mechthild of Magdeburg, Nicolas of Cusa, Jacob Boehme.

Theologically, the emphasis on negative theology loosens the grip of a reified, monarchial monotheism. Monarchial theism can provide a sense of security in a dangerous, even traumatizing world. It can instill a sense of the non-ultimacy of the degradations that assault humanity by protecting an identity irreducible to suffering and humiliation. But monarchial theism easily becomes a defense of hierarchical and authoritarian ideals of human power. It is easy to believe, with Constantine, that "we have received from Divine Providence the supreme favor of being relieved from all error."[15] But this political danger so well described by Laurel Schneider, Catherine Keller, and Mayra Rivera, is accompanied by psycho-spiritual vulnerabilities that are perhaps equally pernicious. In our anxieties it seems natural to project onto the divine the characteristics that we believe would relieve us from vulnerability. We wish for an all-powerful monarch whose power and will are coextensive. The magnificence of this being demands utter loyalty and rejection or even ignorance of "him" casts one beyond the pale. The enemies of God deserve nothing but annihilation or endless suffering. In our anxiety we cling to this false route to security and religion becomes the vehicle for translating hostility toward those unlike us into social and political realities.

The way of negation challenges this construction of power, but it functions at a deeper level to dissolve the attachments that make a monarchial solution to anxiety and suffering so tempting. More than an intellectual discipline, it is a spiritual exercise, undermining not only ideas but dualistic modes of awareness. It is natural that we are deeply habituated to dualistic thinking: language and sense perception, the experience of a body in the world, the distinction we make between self and other which is the basis of relationship are all dualistic. It is inevitable that our understanding and even experiences of the divine will be drawn into the dualistic mental habit through which we negotiate our relationships in the world. Negative theology contests this dualistic mental habit in part by challenging the reduction of divinity to a concept. Of course all theology does this in one way or another. The dramatic mystery of divinity is integral to its very meaning. But conceptual assertion of mystery does not affect the dualistic habit of awareness.

Apophatic theologians move awareness more deeply toward the dissolution of dualistic, conceptual constructs. Thinking, for example, the idea of unity, we begin to apprehend that there can be no concept of unity. All of our

---

[15] Quoted in Schneider, *Beyond Monotheism*, 67.

experiences of one or unity are, if not illusory, at least temporary and partial. A person is one thing, but this one is a virtually infinite set of parts and relations: all of the interior body parts, memories, habits, relationships as mother, daughter, lover, teacher, citizen, bearer of the divine image. This one is endlessly multiple. A nation is constituted by its citizens, geography, history, ideals. An apple exists in relation to the children dividing it or the rotten apples that were thrown away. The unity of any object is arrived at by abstracting it from its interior and exterior multiplicities and relationships.

Oneness only exists in relationship to plurality. To form a concept of pure unity is not possible. As we press toward the metaphor of unity as a divine name we are led to the failure of our ability to form such a concept. This should not drive us toward its opposite—divinity is many, which would simply reassert a binary logic and thus abandon the way of negation. As John Thatamanil argues, this concept, too, disintegrates upon interrogation (Thatamanil, "God as ground, contingency, and relation," 240). Discursive reasoning finds this situation uncomfortable and employs many strategies for reasserting the power of conceptual thinking. Perhaps contemporary debates within postmodern theology maintaining the survival of onto-theology within the *via negativa* reflect this tendency.[16]

The discomfort arising from the dissolution of discursive reasoning is existentially painful. But this dissolution is the opening to the divine abyss. Non-dual awareness travels where cognition cannot go. This awareness makes it existentially possible to bear what the cognitive mind finds so uncanny. What is nauseating to dualistic consciousness is blissful to the apophatic dimension of consciousness. This touch and taste of the infinite (as a youthful Schleiermacher put it) allows us to engage theological practice in a different way. The importance of critiquing theistic formulations takes on a different tone. Naturally, identifying the contributions of Christianity to the logic of domination will remain an enduring responsibility. But the dialectic—spiritual as well as intellectual—between naming and negation weaves the power of negation into names themselves. Naming the divine as one or many, as king or lover, takes on the quality of a caress, a love song, rather than a direct attribution. In this mood, theology can be generous toward the many ways traditions conceive of the divine, encountering them as necessary but limited. Something important is being captured in the Nicene Creed, regardless of how bitter and intolerant the process that generated it. Something important is captured, as well, in Arius' defense of an ecclesial structure rooted in religious practice, local communities and the authority of debate and persuasion.

---

[16] See for example, Martin Laird's "The 'Open Country Whose Name is Prayer: Apophasis, Deconstruction, and Contemplative Practice," *Modern Theology*, Vol. 21 no. 1 (January 2005), 141–55.

This is not to say (with an undergraduate in a class years ago) that Hitler has his truth and I have mine. But it suggests a different way of inhabiting the desire for truth, especially theological truths. The practice of discerning what is true, honorable, just, pure, lovely, gracious, excellent, worthy of praise (cf. Philippians 4:8) rests in the prior practice of non-dual awareness of a depth that relativizes all of our truths, all of our praise. If there is insightfulness to be discovered in Athanasius and Arius, in Augustine and Pelagius, in Barth and Tillich, it is because neither alternative can possess a perfect or unambiguous good. Such a possession remains alien to our human condition. But few things are so unambiguously evil that they have no legitimate insight or perspective. Some things do seem irretrievably evil: genocide, torture, the savaging of beings and their ecosystems seem good candidates. But these limit cases should not be the template for interpreting all reality. The binary of truth and falsehood, good and evil is often misleading, granting too much good to the "right" opinions and obscuring the loveliness, graciousness, and excellence of people or policies or religions that are, at first, alien to us.

Negative theology reshapes not only what we say about the divine, but how we understand what we say. Theological language is poetic, evocative, praising and lamenting. Any direct link between our words and divine reality is impossible and so we are free to lavish loving language on the divine. This makes the habit of exclusionary thinking difficult to sustain. "'Souls who love God,' a Sufi sheikh said a thousand years ago, 'know one another by smell, like horses. Though one be in the East and the other in the West, they still feel joy and comfort in each other's talk, and one who lives in a later generation than the other is instructed and consoled by the words of his friend.'"[17] Apophatic theology is a theory and practice that initiates us into this joy and comfort in the great variety of words, concepts, practices through which lovers of the divine express themselves.

The *via negativa* is also a practice that reshapes our understanding of the human person. Cognition is, like sense experience, an aspect of awareness. But it does not connect us to the deeper truths of our (beyond) being. The valorization of cognition not only distorts our understanding of the divine, it distorts our understanding of ourselves and one another. The polydox authors rightly emphasize the oppressive effects of a "logic of the One." The patriarchalism of this logic suppresses the humanity of women. Its racism and colonialism suppresses the humanity of people of color and of colonies.[18] Its hostility toward sexual pleasure and diversity marginalizes sexual minorities and dehumanizes all practitioners of the arts of sexual pleasure. These are

---

[17] "Introduction," Stephen Mitchell, *Bhagavad Gita: A New Translation* (New York: Three Rivers Press, 2002), 14.

[18] Kristine Suna-Koro's essay "Not With One Voice: Counterpoint of Life, Diaspora, Women, Theology, and Writing," in which she discusses the colonization of Latvia is a useful reminder that colonialism wears many faces. See *Women, Writing, Religion* , edited by Emily Holmes and Wendy Farley (Waco, TX: Baylor University Press, 2011), 207–32.

all ways in which the human spirit is damaged and distorted in the attempt to reduce the practices of being human to a sameness improper both to the divine and the human. This logic has crushed the delicious variety of the human spirit by sending indigenous children to brutal residential schools, outlawing native languages and religious practices, and destroying cultural institutions of the Zulu and Kikuyu. These are tragedies—human and divine—too nightmarish to contemplate. The mind veers away from them, acknowledging the words but fleeing the touch of ravaged bodies and maimed minds, persons, families, and cultures clear-cut in defense of a divine monarch whose blood-lust seems insatiable. The apophatic way vivifies our compassion for these atrocities but it also directs us to a deeper oppression of the human spirit.

The capacity to participate in these overt forms of violence rests in part on the prior violence by which the deep recesses of our psycho-spiritual constitution is maimed. The logic of the One has accompanied Christianity since its inception but is intensified by modern epistemology.[19] This epistemology has allowed us to enjoy many benefits but has also denuded our appreciation of interior castle of the spirit. The rise of the Reformation coincided with the rise of this modern paradigm of knowledge and anthropology, defrauding first Protestants and then Roman Catholics of an intuitive understanding of the apophatic depths of the human being—along with the spiritual dimension of creation. In this context, the early temptation of ecclesial power to align Christianity with right belief became greatly exacerbated, almost reducing faith to belief, augmented by a rather thin gruel of morality, though sometimes seasoned with impulses toward love and social justice. Religion reduces to thought and action, as Schleiermacher complained two hundred years ago, responding even then to the predicament that left religion's despisers to choose between dull orthodoxy and art's spiritual freedom.

Scientists of a certain generation warned mothers against indulging their sentimentality by picking up, coddling, or cooing over children. My grandmother was instructed by her doctor that she must, under no circumstances, feed her new born infant more often than every four hours. No matter how she cried or how the milk leaked, responding to an infant's cries would be psychologically devastating. This is, of course, the very reverse of what is required for mental, spiritual, and physical wellbeing. But it was insisted upon with evangelical fervor as scientific, fact-based, and objectively true. It is an example of the mind-boggling stupidity of authoritarian regimes of knowledge: absolutely certain and completely wrong. It is mirrored in religion by the starvation of the human spirit when religion is reduced to belief

---

[19] See, for example, Laurel Schneider's chapter in *Beyond Monotheism*, "Monotheism, western science, and the theory of everything," or Catherine Keller's *God and Power: Counter-Apocalyptic Journeys* (Minneapolis, MN: Fortress Press. 2005).

and morality. In accepting modernist accounts of mind, Christianity conspires with it to starve the human spirit.

Human beings must have the things we hunger for in order to thrive: food, beauty, wonder and understanding, the engagement of our heart in meaningful actions and efforts. But, created in the divine image, we are more than bodies and minds, more than cognition and ethical action. The tap-root of our beyond being is the bridal chamber where we are united with the divine. Here in the cloud of unknowing the beyond being of the divine is "oned" with the beyond being of our (no) self. Without the means to remember this depth, we are not fully human and we too easily act inhumanly to ourselves, to other people, and to the world.

Christian practice has the means to feed this dimension of spirit. Scripture's mysterious depth, rhythms of liturgy, hymns' combination of poetry and music, all defy translation into cognitive theories or moral action. They are bread and wine to souls thirsty for the divine presence, souls longing to hear their true name. The ordinary kindness and courage of many churchgoers testifies to the efficacy of this regular rhythm of nurture.[20] But in the context of a modernist construction of reality, these divine pharmaceuticals can be subjected to procrustean amputations. Scripture becomes literally true statements of quasi-scientific or moral facts. Liturgy mediates right belief that arms congregants for right moral action (sexual propriety, social justice, caring for community members, voting this way or that). The difficulty is not that people of faith believe things or do things or even (only) that some of the things we believe or do are appalling. The deep wound inflicted is the invitation to understand ourselves as believing, doing things. The divine abyss that endlessly caresses its beloved—creation—becomes itself an object of belief, its livingness imperiled by reduction to qualities that are assented to. Faith becomes cognate to acceptance of germ theory. When we understand human beings to be primarily thinkers and actors, we lose our ability to touch and taste the infinite. This wound, so exacerbated by modern epistemology, is tended by apophatic theology. Both the theology and the practice of the divine darkness challenges the temptation to idolize our beliefs about God. But the way of unknowing is not primarily about scolding. It waters us with a memory of who we are, what theology might be, and the sweetness of non-dual love. It allows us to inhabit scripture, liturgy, prayer, belief, ethical commitments with a lightness and joy-

---

[20] I myself write as one who has lost the consolation of liturgy. Like a betrayed lover, I find the simple and delicious trust and intimacy has been shattered and I cannot quite rest in an embrace that is sometimes erotic, sometimes wounding. It is difficult to do justice to all of the ways the church functions in human lives. Its wounding power would seem to discredit it—but it does not. The sweetness of its redemption would seem to make it a good and faithful lover, but it is not. Like wheat and tares, these simply grow up together. But the good householder rejects the servants' suggestion to tear up the tares, insisting they must grow up together. Accepting the difficult mystery of ambiguity is another practice of apophatic (and polydox) theology.

ousness. They are news of the divine but need not bear the heavy weight of being divine. The anxiety that longs for certainty, clarity, total reliability, and total security is quelled. The spirit is able to receive consolation that the ego finds difficult.

Multiplicity as Divine Name

A common metaphor for divinity is the One. Much of the novelty of the polydox writers is their unrepentant celebration of multiplicity. These authors play with this metaphor in a variety of ways. Laurel Schneider appeals to "divine multiplicity" as the context for affirming an ethics of love.[21] Catherine Keller stretches language in fascinating ways, concluding her magnificent work with the *tehomic* icon, "a plurisingularity of universe, earth echoing chaos, dark deep vibrating spirit."[22] Mayra Rivera identifies God as the "beginning of diversity," as "that multiple singularity that joins together all creatures—creatures that are themselves irreducible in the infinite multiplicity of their own singularity."[23] They do not put it this way, but one might borrow from Pseudo-Dionysius and say that for them multiplicity is an important name of God. Names are not literal designations. From an apophatic perspective, neither one nor many, neither unity nor multiplicity would constitute direct or univocal affirmations about God's *being*. The celebration of multiplicity is a corrective not so much to monotheism *per se* as to the logic of the One that so often distorts it. Through the practice of negative theology, the adequacy of all binary thinking is challenged. Divinity does not reduce to an either/or, a hierarchical valorization of logics of a one or of multiplicity. Conceptuality splinters non-duality into dualistic categories but reification of either side of a binary or the binary itself is incompatible with non-conceptual, non-essential reality of divinity. The emphasis on multiplicity corrects the distortion that occurs when One is literalized. This corrective, like the other elements of the *via negativa*, is not only a critique but also an opening onto the deep wisdom of the Christian tradition. It is both an integral aspect of Christian theology and a timely recovery of the plenitude of being as we consider the pluralities represented not only by marginalized human beings but also by other religions and nature itself. That is, celebration of multiplicity is a crucial dimension of devotion to the Beloved. Through it, we "make a way out of (the) no way" of the logic of the One.[24] Rooting multiplicity in traditional resources and contemporary reconfigurations

---

[21] Schneider, *Beyond Monotheism*, 202.

[22] Keller, *Face of the Deep*, 238.

[23] Marya Rivera, *Touch of Transcendence: a Postcolonial Theology of God* (Louisville, KY: Westminster John Knox Press, 2007), 137.

[24] Monica Coleman offers a particularly powerful and imaginative incorporation of a variety of sources into theology not only in her essay in the *Polydoxy* volume but in her longer work, *Making a Way Out of No Way: a Womanist Theology* (Minneapolis, MN: Fortress Press, 2008).

opens a path between devotion and compassionate action. In these senses, multiplicity does become (in Dionysius's sense) a name of the divine.

Polydoxy echoes the wisdom expressed by the writers of Job and the Psalms, by Plato and Plotinus: divinity spins off an endless variety of beauty, cherishing the morning stars, the womb of the sea, light and darkness, wild weather, calving mountain goats, the predatory hawk, the massive Leviathan and Behemoth.[25] The Good beyond Being is essenceless, a divine emptiness because its radiant self-manifestation draws into ordered, beautiful being everything that exists in any way whatsoever. To love the Good is to open one's heart to the vastness of cosmic wonder, to a "touch of transcendence" (as Mayra Rivera puts it in her delightfully oxymoronic phrase).[26] Multiplicity is such a small word to capture this erotic, exuberant energy which is equally at home in the vast nothingness between galaxies, the explosion of stars, the strangely toxic atmosphere of Venus, the tenderness of a hind protecting its fawn, the hunger of a young lion, the ordered procession of the stars, the chaos of a refugee camp or storm.

> I permeate all the universe
> In my unmanifest form.
> All beings exist within me
> Yet I am so inconceivably
> Vast, so beyond existence . . .

Bhagavad Gita 9.4, 14

Meditation on this great cosmic and temporal dance of life and death is an important antidote to the somewhat pinched habit of Christian piety to conceive of the divine presence only on this earth, in our religion, in the portion of our religion with which we are most sympathetic.

Multiplicity recovers what may be the most characteristic effect of divine power. The physical cosmos, the multi-dimensional regions of mind, the absurd proliferation of flora and fauna testify to a bewildering and mind-blowing range of existents. To think of the cultural diversities through which humanity has organized meaning or even the interior complexity of a single human mind is to come up against a task infinite in scope. If the world is the effect of divine creativity, it is difficult to imagine that the endless zest and beauty of wild abundance is not a reflection of something cherished (to speak anthropomorphically) by the divine life. To make one's life an unending hymn to this endless love surely must also involve loving what is created by this inexhaustible source: Holy Wisdom is "more mobile than any motion; because of her pureness she pervades and penetrates all things. She is the

---

[25] Catherine Keller's *Face of the Deep* is perhaps the most "systematic" development of multiplicity as a primary name of divine reality.
[26] Mayra Rivera, *The Touch of Transcendence: A Postcolonial Theology of God* (Louisville, KY: Westminster John Knox Press, 2007).

breath of the power of God, and a pure emanation of the glory of the Almighty" (Wisdom of Solomon 8:24–25). The way of Wisdom participates in Her cherishing of other beings, the wisdom of other religions, the beauty of nature. This way is far removed from the dull duty of inclusive piety or the exigency of tolerance. It is a chant of praise.

From Theory to Practice

I began in lament and near despair and end in praise. Polydoxy is an academic enterprise. As academics, scholars, church people, we need intellectual resources such as this one to challenge assumptions and refresh our appreciation of the many rivers that flow through our faith. But the work of our time requires more than new theological insights, however exciting and important. I sometimes feel that these writers are afraid of what they are uncovering. These wonderful, playful, creative, morally passionate writers are academic theologians—as am I—but what should we do? As these writers themselves also convey, polydoxy does not culminate in academic papers and symposia. It leaps its own levies, flowing onto parched land, land dying for relief. The polydox, the fellow travelers, will put aside journals like this one, leave their libraries and computers and go into the world.

> You have a right to your actions,
> But never to your action's fruits.
> Act for action's sake.
> And do not be attached to inaction . . .
> The wise [person] lets go of all
> Results, whether good or bad,
> And is focused on the action alone.
> Yoga is skill in actions.
>
> *Bhagavad Gita* 1.47, 51

For Gandhi, who remained devoted to this Song all of his life, this is its crucial wisdom. "I have felt that in trying to enforce in one's life the central teaching of the Gita, one is bound to follow truth and *ahimsa* [nonviolence]. When there is no desire for fruit, there is no temptation for untruth or *himsa* [violence]. Take any instance of untruth or violence, and it will be found that behind it was the desire to attain the cherished end."[27] As the oceans collapse and drought tortures the Horn of Africa, as people already die from toxic air pollution, and thousands of species careen down the ramp to extinction, we act as best we can. Like Arjuna on the field of battle in the opening scene of the *Gita*, we anticipate the savage devastation that is upon us. Like him we

---

[27] Mohandas K. Gandhi, "The Message of the Gita," Appendix, *Bhagavad Gita*, 218.

may feel paralyzed and implore the Incarnate One to guide us: "Krishna, my mind is utterly confused. Tell me where my duty lies, which path I should take. I am your pupil; I beg for instruction. For I cannot imagine how any victory . . . could drive away this grief that is withering my senses" (*Bhagavad Gita* 2). Krishna displays for him the larger cosmic and divine body in which his actions occur. War is real and also a metaphor for what is most hopelessly brutal in the human condition. Krishna insists we must act in this struggle as heroes and yet remain mindful that our ultimate context is divine. In this sphere of reality we act but we do not control the fruit of our action. It belongs to us to act heroically in the struggle for the earth and for justice. But it does not belong to us to control empires. It belongs to us to act well and pray well, without paralyzing attachment to success or failure. As Teresa of Avila says: "Let nothing disturb you, let nothing affright you. All things are passing . . .Who has God wants nothing. God alone suffices."[28] Or, to return to the wisdom of the Gita:

> [The truly wise] always chanting my praise,
> Steadfast in their devotion
> They make their lives an unending
> Hymn to my endless love.
>
> *Bhagavad Gita* 9:14

The forest outside my window was clear-cut three times. Each time the glory of that amazing tree community was utterly destroyed, carted away so that nothing remained but dry earth and stubble. But each time a forest came back. Not as healthy, but yearning to live. The forest embodies an urgent drive to live. To be. To be beautiful, each being individually and each co-present with the other life forces of the forest, a song of mutuality. Like the forest, let us ever chant devotion to the Beloved: in our action and our inaction, our prayer, our petitions, our despair, laments, and resurging hope, let us surrender to the bonds of compassion and ignite our mutual joy.

---

[28] This is referred to simply as Teresa of Avila's bookmark, because she supposedly carried it in her prayer book.

Modern Theology 30:3 July 2014
ISSN 0266-7177 (Print)
ISSN 1468-0025 (Online)

DOI: 10.1111/moth.12125

GETTING IT RIGHT

LAUREL C. SCHNEIDER

This is a delight. Many of the authors in this special issue take seriously
Rubenstein's and Tanner's invitation to engage their own generative thinking
alongside or with whatever idea of "polydoxy" they see developed in the
volume Catherine and I edited together by that name. Reading them, I have
been challenged to think more seriously about the intimate relation between
polydoxy and orthodoxy, a challenge that I take up in this response, not in
order to quell concerns, but in order to take them as seriously as they are
voiced in some of the articles here. But before I move into that question I must
say that I also found myself at some points stopped in my tracks by the
poetry, depth and invitation of some of these essays. For example Wendy
Farley, whose intuitions of multiplicity and relation far outstrip my own,
suggests that polydoxy "leaps its own levies, flowing onto parched land, land
dying for relief." She goes on to claim that "the polydox, the fellow travellers,
will put aside journals like this one, leave their libraries and computers and
go into the world." Of course, she sits at her computer to write those words,
and knows the paradox of what she says. That is the beauty of it. She understands at a deep level that whatever "polydoxy" is about, it is not either-or
thinking or doing, even when entrenched habits of critique lead to such
well-trod paths of worry. And as Mark Jordan so precisely declares in
response to the creeping necrosis he diagnoses in theological thinking of late
(to which he sees the efforts described by polydoxy as a potential step in the
direction of life): "I want to say: The arduous purpose of theological writing
is luring readers into forms of speech that none of you has been taught to
read, much less to speak."

So, after an anthology dedicated to the name and now a collection of
conversations with it, what is *polydoxy*? To be sure, it is a funny-sounding

Laurel C. Schneider
Department of Religious Studies, Vanderbilt University, 2301 Vanderbilt Place, 301A Garland
Hall, Nashville, TN 37235, USA
Email: laurel.c.schneider@vanderbilt.edu

word that might have come from the pen of Theodor Geisel, along with
oobleck, Whoville, Yertle, and the Lorax. Unfamiliar on the tongue, polydoxy
seems to prove a bit of a stretch for the imagination as well. When we
solicited the essays for the 2011 volume, Catherine and I went around and
through several clusters of possibilities for a title that would usefully posit
the nature of the work without setting up an unnecessary negative (hence, for
example, we rejected all options that began with "post" or even "beyond"),
and when Catherine suggested *polydoxy,* we knew immediately that the word
itself, in its intentional overlap with orthodoxy, would prove clear in its
leanings toward multiplicity. Because of this, I confess to being mildly surprised by responses that consider polydoxy to indicate some kind of binary
opposition to orthodoxy or suggest that polydoxy depends upon a necessary
polemic regarding the orthodox in making its case for multiplicity and relation. But of course, just because a binary, strident, opposition is not *necessary*
in polydoxy's constructive move does not mean that such opposition does
not reassert itself or come into play in the process of grasping the unfamiliar
parameters of speech that none of us have been taught to read.

There is dangerous hubris in claiming to have discovered a new thought.
The danger is multiple: forgetting that new things are not ever new to every-
one, forgetting that a new thought is never *ex nihilo,* and so not new in itself,
really, and forgetting that whatever displacement a new thing or thought or
practice may entail, the displaced is not gone. I encounter new things and
new thoughts all the time, new to me, flowing from the generosity of the
world and of colleagues, and of life. Newness is the party frock (or horror
mask) of change and growth, a sometimes lovely, sometimes devastating
presentation, but it is utterly contextual. And so I want to clarify that
"polydoxy" is new, but in name only and even then, as Jordan points out, not
really. Furthermore, it is a provisional name for a complex of approaches and
ideas that are not new in themselves, but may be new in their reception under
this particular umbrella term. Polydoxy is new only in the shorthand naming
of a pre-existing momentum of scholarly exchange and poetic intuition that
includes a wide swath of contemporary writers in theological philosophy,
ethics, and historical studies.

Despite this caveat of non-new newness, the fact that a perception of
opposition between (new) polydoxy and (pre-existing) orthodoxy exists for
some after reading the anthology means that those of us who find ourselves
in the cluster of approaches that fit under the nominal umbrella of
"polydoxy"—or theologies of multiplicity and relation—have more work to
do if the shorthand, playful nickname for our work is to be useful and not
merely distracting. And that is all it should be, useful. But useful for what?
For whom? Useful in part, as Jordan posits, for a committed decolonial effort
that "means imagining anti-imperial characters and communities [and traces
of the divine?] without succumbing to the fantasy that finding the right
words will magically embody them." Useful in part for working our various

ways through what Farley describes with aching accuracy as "lost consolation". The "for whom" is implied in the "for what"—for the betrayed lovers of Christian worship, for the excluded, hell-condemned (which, as I argue in *Beyond Monotheism*, can be read as a synonym for "embodied"), for the oppressed and colonized, for the scientifically curious, spiritually restless and poetically minded. Of course none of these "for whoms" sets up an opposition, as if every other theological intuition is somehow against them. But most of all, at this point perhaps "polydoxy" is for the guild of theologians, especially for those of us who are dissatisfied, restless, still in love with the inherited stories, practices, and traditions albeit a little—or a lot—betrayed. It is for those of us in the guild not yet ready to walk away entirely, perhaps persuaded that there is no choosing to leave as Clayton Crockett so provocatively suggests. This insight about choice may also illuminate the shared worry over the name "polydoxy." Choosing a new name is always vulnerable to the fallacy of purity and so to becoming a "rallying cry," as Burrus notes, behind which easily march ugly armies, and a taste for blood.

If the name does not overly distract from the rich theological possibilities of multiplicity and relation that it abbreviates, then for some "polydoxy" is a methodological means for holding together the interstitial complexity and porosity of the texts and traditions that undergird every orthodoxy. For others it is a useful preferential option for texts and traditions that have embedded within them—and have had embedded all along—creative instabilities and anti-imperial, decolonial traces. Or "polydoxy" may be useful as a manifesto of sorts: of praise for and commitment to embodied, sensuous and complex creaturely difference (but needing Jordan's caution all the while to be cautious of the tendency—constitutive inevitability?—of manifestos to betray their own cause). For still others of us "polydoxy" marks a posture of openness, a practice of non-reduction and non-duality, an aesthetic and ethical preference for poetry, ambiguity, *sans*, receptivity and movement in theological construction and systematization. From where I sit, "polydoxy" gestures toward and welcomes all of these descriptions—and certainly more. All to the good! But the question remains: how are these strategies and commitments opposed to orthodoxy? Perhaps they are, but only if orthodoxy is very narrowly conceived as a stable signifier of something monolithic and unchanging, something that every author agrees it is not.

Although I would like to be done with it, I am conscious of the seriousness of the concern regarding polydoxy as some kind of David to an orthodoxy-Goliath. The worry on behalf of orthodoxy is real, namely that we not conceive of it so narrowly that it becomes a caricature. And the concern for those of us engaged in the work called polydoxy is also real, that we not inadvertently reinscribe the very rigidities that we are working so hard to massage back into life under the imagined—and false—purity of the new. The fact of collegial concern has made me realize that, while I have not wanted to spend much energy on the question of orthodoxy, either to save it or to condemn it, I am reminded again and again of the fantasy of that wish so long as I intend to speak with and to theologians, and so long as I intend to claim and sympathetically read my own rich inheritance of ancient texts, traditions, and practices.

I have already limned polydoxy as I understand and work within it, and it is time to think more clearly about polydoxy's intimate relation to orthodoxy, to clarify its non-competitive relation, at least to a most basic definition of the latter. But that is the issue. What does "orthodoxy" mean when we worry about it? I understand orthodoxy—along with several modern English and classical Greek dictionaries—to mean "right" or "correct" praise (or doctrine, or thinking, or even practice when orthopraxy is at lunch). "Right" of course implies its own opposition, namely "wrong." So does this constitutive opposition in the linguistic structure of orthodoxy necessitate that anything other than "ortho" in the prefix to "doxa" means "wrong" or "incorrect"? Furthermore, if we are proposing "polydoxy" as a clarification and complication of right praise, doctrine or thinking, is it not then, by definition, orthodoxy? How can polydoxy be opposed to orthodoxy so defined? It is frankly incoherent for the authors of the original *Polydoxy* collection of essays to argue for something that they consider wrong praise, wrong doctrine, or wrong thinking.

But of course orthodoxy does not, cannot, stay quietly in its place in the dictionary under the category of "right" and "correct." It lurks like a bored teenager itching for trouble around entries like power, institution, empire, university, discipline, and church. Orthodoxy has sidled up to rulers of all sorts and proven useful to them in institutional contexts where rules of privilege matter. This is because "ortho-" as "right-" is capacious, an empty vessel just waiting to be filled with specific, contextual, content. Hence its lexical restlessness. And as a number of writers here and in the original volume argue, "ortho-" too often morphs into "status-quo-" or even "imperial-" and as such must be opposed on behalf of the oppressed. *That* orthodoxy is opposable in a binary sense, I suppose, but we are no longer talking about *ortho*doxy but a particular content of normativity that we must oppose or become utter hypocrites. In particular, we are talking about the specific content of "right" in the context of imperial Christianity that became and still becomes viciously wrong praise, wrong doctrine, wrong thinking. Are we not?

"Orthodoxy" has been deployed historically as a hammer of empire, a tool of ecclesial management, and an organizing principle in hotly contested pluralistic environments. In much of her published work as well as her article here, Virginia Burrus is particularly helpful in clarifying the difference between orthodoxies deployed then and now. With the precision of a restorer of ancient masterpieces, she peels back the layers of rhetoric both ancient and contemporary without letting go of their complex influences on present questions, in this case the question of polydoxy. My suggestion here (new to me but not, I am sure, to the multitude of philologists and historians of orthodoxy) that orthodoxy's content is ultimately empty underscores Burrus' argument that there is no stable orthodoxy in any time or place. Indeed, she suggests that this is polydoxy's point.

So which orthodoxy does polydoxy oppose, and which does it clarify? I hope that it opposes nominal orthodoxies whose specific content of "right" results in the denial of constitutive multiplicity and the reification of status quo hierarchies of oppression and practices of torture. This is a fairly uncontroversial hope, or so I hope! I also hope that polydoxy clarifies ortho-doxies whose content of "right" is a "skillful means" of love that leads to complex thriving of the world and all of its creatures and to liberation of the oppressed. Polydoxy's opposition, I then conclude, is to orthodoxy that is neither right nor correct, and so not orthodox anyway. Polydoxy as an umbrella term is useful, I suggest, only so long as it clarifies the constitutive and responsive multiplicity of what we understand—for now—to be "right" and "good" and even "true" and so giving content to "orthodoxy." To borrow from Catherine Keller's helpful rubric in her introductory volume *On the Mystery*, this understanding of multiplicity of rightness is neither dissolute (in which everything must be right, so there is no possible distinction between right and wrong) nor absolute (in which multiplicity is an incoher-ently unyielding many that excludes oneness entirely) but it *is* resolute, allowing for a clarity about the rightness and meaning of love that—even in their complexity—can distinguish suffering from flourishing, violence from peace, oppression from liberation.

In conclusion I should say that I have been writing this response far from my academic habitat. I am on supposed vacation and so I am inclined to brevity lest I miss yet another morning in this too-brief span of time to walk along the shore with nothing but the abyssal glory of the ocean at my side. I can hear it from where I sit, though, along with the cacophonous jabber of so many avian discourses. Despite my impatience, being without the benefit of any academic library or even the fallback of internet, I enjoy this opportunity to think on what these colleagues have offered, to reflect more rather than read more, to listen rather than research more. And though I am eager to follow Farley's advice to the polydox and leave my computer for, in my case, the busy commerce of creatures and waves at the salty lip of land, I will hold still a bit longer to express gratitude for the wisdom resident in all of the essays: counsel to step lightly lest beautiful inheritances be crushed for no good reason beyond the lure of the new, offerings of wider multiplicities through narrower passages (I am thinking here of Linn Tonstad's reflection on the Trinity), and gentle pushes toward more than thought.

The questions that I carry with me, that enhance the projects of all of the authors in both collections, are the ones that speak to the challenges of doing this work in ways that do not "proclaim to supersede what has come before" but that stretch what has come before into skins that we can inhabit. Or that give us some "different way[s] of inhabiting the desire for truth, especially theological truths." That keep us "faithful to the blindness" that structures our sight and patiently resistant to temptations of elevation "into a scripture never to be rivaled." Whether under the name polydoxy or something else, the questions of complex worldly relation and theological imagining of incarnate divinity within that complexity and multiplicity are alive and growing. They do not indicate something other, or even new, but gesture toward a theological sensibility that follows a kind of intuitive plumb line. Maybe what results from all of this is even right from time to time.

Modern Theology 30:3 July 2014
ISSN 0266-7177 (Print)
ISSN 1468-0025 (Online)

DOI: 10.1111/moth.12126

"THEOLOGY'S MULTITUDE: POLYDOXY REVIEWED AND RENEWED"

CATHERINE KELLER

The conversation that materialized in the volume *Polydoxy* arose as a reflection on and within multiplicity. We needed to think about religious, social and ecological difference all together, in a multiplicity of multiplicities, and so to reconsider the vectors and voices that have rent and energized theology in this epoch. We needed, beyond the competing grievances of our variant constituencies, to ask—and to ask theologically—about multiplicity itself. What matters about it, how does it demand and exceed pluralism? Of course our answers vary. The name "polydoxy" is hardly an answer, but at best a place-holder. As Mark Jordan notes, the word's ancient meaning signals "diversity of opinion," and—wonderfully—"multiply praised". Polydoxy remains semantically too old and too new to contain any of our work. But perhaps in this we concur: that the members of a multiplicity are held in inescapable relation to each other's difference. If—unlike a mere plurality—the many making up a multi*pli*city fold, *pli*, in and out of one another, then each member enfolds its exterior and is reciprocally enfolded. So difference (signifies) not separateness but relationship itself. Neither distance nor competition, neither irrelevance nor malevolence, neither transcendence nor immanence, erases relationship. In the perspective we have experimentally called polydoxy, difference multiplies just where the boundary between inside and out comes into question. The illumining diversity of responses composing the present collection press the question further, harder, with a complicating generosity.

Catherine Keller
Theological School, Drew University, 36 Madison Avenue, Madison NJ 07940, USA
Email: ckeller@drew.edu

Still, the Other has its romance and its ethics: the Exterior invites exodus, escape—and not only up toward a transcendent infinity. "The thrilling *dehors*" [Bataille], transcendence of an oppressive world, or of the Sartrean hell of "other people at breakfast": its interior may come under the sign of *no exit*. The relations in its within may turn infernal. But the hell that polydoxy flees, perhaps indeed transcends, is not that of relationality *per se*, but of its collapse into uniformity, into an enclosure whose unity is won by disconnection from its exterior. A constitutive exclusion founds a homogenizing inclusion. Then it seems that one can only escape the fused oneness through another flight—existential, spiritual, transgressive, exceptional. One wants *out*.

If, however, there is after all no simple unity In Here, then there is no merely transcendent Out There. Or more bluntly: short of fantasy or death, there is no escaping the relations that make us up. But we may ignore them. Or we may alter them dramatically. The legacies, for example of gendered, sexed, racialized, classed relationships, will not be simply left behind—even at the Rapture; but we do know in our time and in our flesh their alteration and their press for yet greater alteration. There is no escaping the earth. But we might alter the way we are earthlings together. And oh we'd better, soon. There is, furthermore, at least within Euroamerican civilization, no escaping Christianity, no matter what hells it has hosted. And because we mind the effects of those exclusive inclusions—for heaven's sake, let us not flee the resources of the redemptively embodied and branching relationality of whose multiplicity we remain members.

Are we then talking as and to members of the body of Christ, really, here? Who *are* we speaking to, some of our respondents have reasonably asked? Indeed the Christian theologians who compose most but not all of both volumes on polydoxy are calling out the ecclesia. They summon it precisely not as a bounded body, a body sealed in the supersessionist skin of its exclusions—first of its Jews and its pagans—but as the opened, wounded body minding the shifting diversity of relations that have made it up all along. The queered, opened body of Christ is trying to find its decolonial way to offer back to its others—inside and out—something of what it had "cribbed" from them (in Schneider's natal pun) from the start (Schneider, "Crib notes from Bethlehem," 19ff.). But what is returned will not be the same. In *Polydoxy* we were writing to those already worrying about how one receives, how one gives, the gift of a Christian way now wrapped for two millennia in colonized and colonizing clichés of itself. This way that can for a certain stretch be called polydoxy can be neither identical with "the Christian Way"—as though there ever was *one*—nor separable from it.

To articulate such a nonseparable difference as a theological method remains the treacherous test of multiplicity itself. Nonseparable—or, as I prefer now to call it, *entangled* difference, names the abstract width of the utter concreteness of a socio-ontology of relation. All relations matter, many materialize, but few are called—into attention, repetition and emphasis. We are wondering how in the Christian incarnation an entangling difference materialized, how it selects amidst multiplicity and how it *matters* now, when the earth and its wounded populations call us out, *inside out*, of the squabbling, privileged enclosures that become ever more tempting.

As we had insisted earlier: "The relation of a subject to an inexchangeable other, itself already related to other inexchangeable others, is what makes possible the plural manifestations of worldly experience. This descriptive truth takes on normative force. Relationality distinguishes pluralism from the relativism that swamps judgment and inhibits resolution."[1] Happily none of our readers have here accused us of relativism, though the whirring, pulsing, over-extending relativity in which subjects take place, in which ethics unfolds, does undo every absolutism. But the unbounded width, the universalizing claims, of this relationality—yes, we are entangled with the universe itself—will themselves after all tempt us to our own overstatements, our indeconstructible deconstructions, our absolute relativisms, our relationality absolute of the singular event of relation. Absolutely.

I am trying to say something about the philosophy of this project, something that in its content is as concrete as it is abstract. For the abstract formulation—of the experience of our multiplicitous connectivity, of that which I unfold elsewhere as *the nonseparable difference of an apophatic entanglement*—is an effect not of rational purgation of particularity but of the effort to enfold impossible diversities in possible language. Every ontology, cosmology, metaphysics, indeed every theology makes the effort to encompass a world of contentious relations. And perhaps every such universal discourse is doomed to betray its earthy, fragile patch of the universe. To betray in both senses: to reveal and to be disloyal to that concrete multiplicity. Of course that is why the resort to a localism, a particularism of multiple discrete contexts, might seem more true to polydoxy. But nonseparable difference won't rest there. It cannot. Each context, each singularity, bleeds into its neighbors.

A rigorous teaching of multiplicity must bear the press of the whole universe into language; it must therefore face as its own universalism's temptations to flight, or to power. That means it must occasionally confess its own incomprehension; it must remind itself in language of the incapacity of its language.

Then it may honestly bear witness, urgent witness, to particular relations, at a particular place and time, urging particular priority. And it does so knowing there is no extricating these particulars from their cosmoi of impinging relations. The particularity of, for instance, the Christ event, never did settle the question of priorities—it only intensified it. As local event its

---

[1] Catherine Keller and Laurel Schneider, (eds), *Polydoxy: Theology of Multiplicity and Relation* (New York: Routledge, 2011), 9. Subsequent references to *Polydoxy* will be cited internally by author, title, and page number.

resonances (neither Jew nor Greek, slave nor free, man nor woman) were from the start polyglossal, cosmopolitan, counterimperial—but with such a universalizing intensity as to eventuate in imperial appropriation. Beyond moments of illumination, Christianity boundlessly amplified the temptations of flight and power right along with the openings to cosmopolitan alterity. No impatient indignation will solve this ambiguity.

I am in other words grateful for this opportunity to rehearse that which by way of a method, a relation of those *met hodos*, "together on a way," we practice in communicating with each other, and so with each of the others—the gracious, divergent others—enfolded in the present text and now willingly tangled in polydoxy itself. *Polydoxy* itself, in case it does for a moment name something worth doing, must admit to being *a* way, really more or less one, that mindfully crosses, accompanies or converges with other ways, some more intimately than others. So for example our subtitle was "theology of multiplicity and relation," not "theologies." Laurel Schneider and I recognized that for this moment, this conversation, we have to do with *a* multiplicity, and more particularly, with a singular proposal for enfolding multiplicity in general. A way, a path through the aporetic, not just one among endless possible directions trailing off into the wasteland. It never claims to be *the* Way. But most of us do not wander far from *ho hodos*. There is no essay in the original collection that does not Christologically resonate with, for instance, Mayra Rivera's way of rereading the Johannine *doxa*, its glory—"as long as its divinity keeps materializing in earthly grounds, becoming vulnerable flesh" (Rivera, "Glory: the first passion of theology?," 180).

Just what polydoxy *is* at this point (a nonpunctual point, a moment of shifting convergences) or what it *was* at some point of origin (a conference? or the sum of millennia of antecedents enfolded into that conversation?) will only matter from a perspective that has not yet quite *come to be*. That to-come, which is already becoming, that *advenire* (I write on the second Sunday in Advent) signifies an opening into an unknown that has not been nor ever will be mastered. The becoming of an apophatically entangled perspective signals no smooth and predictable emergence, but rather the abysmal uncertainty as to the future of theology, of Christianity, and of the earth that contains them. At the same time it enfolds that uncertainty nonseparably within an infinite indeterminacy—the "cloud of unknowing"—that has not left us quite clueless.

We do not however confuse clues with certainty, or faith with knowledge. Faith seeking understanding is after all *still seeking*—if it is still faith. No matter how often the church repeats "I believe in God the Father Almighty," an ancient *symbolon* of faith will not morph into knowledge that, say, God is an omnipotent patriarch. Much has been understood along the way, the Way. And we lose it when we think we've *got* it. Then understanding congeals into the understood; it no longer wanders the way, it has arrived. Since we learn much, we do accumulate knowledge; since we recall endless arrivals and enjoy new ones, the cataphatic is always tempted to trump the apophatic. And the apophatic may then reactively empty into the aporetic (with its thrilling *dehors*). But waylessness is no more on the way than is finality. We who pursue our experiments in polydoxy are surely tempted to both—to a relativist void and to our own relationalist counter-certainties. It would be truly clueless to imagine that these binary risks could be avoided. But they *can* be recognized.

The clues to the enfolding mystery build up criteria for the discernment of more clues. We defined the polydox not as *multiplicity* alone but joined triadically with its *relationality* and the *unknown*. That uncertainty marks the indeterminacy of *becoming*. To be on the way is to be in process, in a becoming that is *known* to signify the not-yet and therefore the not yet knowable of what is still to come. The *love* that reveals the relations, the *justice* that honors the diversities, the *apophasis* that breaks speech open to a logos that exceeds it: these criteria do not stand still. They stand, but they tremble. They tremble, but they stand. They support faithful co-productions of fresh knowledge. They stir cosmopolitical action. They seem—right. Right on. Right enough.

So are we after all pursuing some new right-teaching, destined to supersede the prior truth-regime? Or do we offer some cunningly entangled, postmodern variant of the original Christian orthodoxy? Either way, a new orthodoxy? Some of our interlocutors in this special issue worry—casting not a single anathema—about this possible crypto-orthodoxy. The historian of early Christianity Virginia Burrus cuts with irenic elegance to the heart of the problem. She wonders whether in the name of polydoxy we have "not so much deconstructed the discourse of orthodoxy as inverted it, thereby making a heresy of orthodoxy and instating polydoxy as . . . well, yet another orthodoxy announcing the triumph over false belief—or rather, in this case, the triumph over the falseness of belief as such." She is asking, not accusing. But if the answer (beyond her text, which doesn't give one) turns out to be affirmative, then of course we are performing a creative destruction rather than deconstruction, and sabotaging the better angels of our multiplicity. Similarly, if from the converse direction, Graham Ward asks—not just rhetorically—"whether 'polydoxy' is working with a reified understanding of 'orthodoxy' in order to construct a position from which to announce its own distinctiveness?"

These are indispensable questions, generically crucial to the unfolding of any project like ours, whether or not it would call upon the name of polydoxy. It is indeed uncertain whether any project that does not confine itself either to history or to revival of historic doctrine can avoid all slippage from announcing to pronouncing, from disclosure to a new closure. Hopefully we unsay such slips rapidly enough. The entire challenge of a relationality of difference, of the difference that relationality makes when it avows itself, lies here: the righting of relation surely *seeks* an orthopraxis and in some unsettling sense means always to speak rightly. We are always trying to get it right. Yet to "be" orthodox is to *have* it right. So we might need to admit this much: *polydoxy as a term, a name, a sign is parasitical on orthodoxy*. As a name polydoxy has no position, no pulse or panache, without its difference from (and thus relation to) living avowals of orthodoxy—classical, retro-, neo- or radical. As a theological neologism, polydoxy tags a couple of millennia behind orthodoxy. But as content it is not only dependent upon orthodoxy but entangled with it. For it is positioned within a discursive field—a multiplicity—largely shaped and hosted by a mainline of western Christian theology.

That mainline, even in its liberal and liberationist forms, hews as close as possible to the ancient orthodoxy and eschews as much as possible those positions, those constitutive exclusions, defined as heretical. No historian has demonstrated the constitutive character of the heretic for the orthodox better than Burrus.[2] We in that mainline may and do protest certain exclusions, we may and do protest the originative authority granted a mechanism of exclusion by which inclusion is defined. We may demonstrate that, as Judith Butler shows of sexuality and Agamben of political sovereignty, the excluded exception is in fact always included. But by that same token we too remain part of a multiplicity that includes and is itself theologically shaped by orthodoxy, including its exclusions. If many of our key sources are either older or other than any form of Christian theology—then that of course must also be said of the sources of Christian theology in general. Hence we insist (offering a complement that may or may not be accepted) upon the polydoxical condition of Christian orthodoxy.

It seems that we cannot simultaneously position ourselves within Christian theology *and* claim some sort of virtuous transcendence of the history of orthodoxy, let alone of its exclusions—as though one transcends merely by criticizing. Or as though altering what it means to do theology thereby frees us from the constituent condition. This ambiguous condition may mount at any moment into the "writing terror" Mark Jordan so vividly tracks: "the imperial terrors that theology can authorize, but perhaps even more the solitary terrors of a blank page not yet written in a language that no one now is quite able to speak." And though we do not call ourselves orthodox, we cannot avoid divergence among ourselves about when or whether we are *inside* of Christianity or about which openings *within* Christian language make it more porous, developmental, and even multiple than it might seem—often as signaled by thinkers *outside* of the Christian fold. Of course this inside-out circumstance of polydoxy itself requires recurrent justification, argument, agonism. After all, the very rhetoric and verve of orthodoxy, even when it refrains from anathemas, stems from ancient practices of

---

[2] Virginia Burrus, *The Making of a Heretic: Gender, Authority, and the Priscillianist Controversy* (Berkeley, CA: University of California Press, 1995), and Virginia Burrus, *Begotten Not Made: Conceiving Manhood in Late Antiquity* (Stanford, CA: Stanford University Press, 2000).

debate, without which there has not been nor will be any discourse that can be called "theology." The pagan sources of theology determine this condition. There may be a scriptural Logos but no "ology" without critical engagements among the "diversity of opinions."

In order to articulate our difference (as entangled nonseparably and so perhaps all the more annoyingly) from avowed orthodoxies we will therefore in the mode of argument no doubt sometimes mirror and mock their oppositionalism. We will offend their defenses, we will defend our own offenses. And when, further, we resort to hostile simplifications, to polemical cartoons, we not only repay but replay, in style if not in content, the exclusionary sort of orthodoxy we disclaim. These are sins we may confess even if we cannot stamp them out. Even so, it remains unclear whether Ward will or can accept the gift we offer—unless a gracious response counts ipso facto as reception.

If however my defense of polydoxy bends further backward, confessing yet more failures of our love and double standards of our complication, admitting even the Trojan horseplay of our gift, I may appear to surrender to a toxic logic. Toxic, at least, for us: that to oppose the anathematizing power of our own heritage is to reinscribe it; to avoid the anathemas we must thus acquiesce to them.

Oh dear. Any doxy may turn toxic. Perhaps we can just hope that the poison, the *Gift*, produces here its immunological effects.

I'd give up now if this were not such a familiar dilemma, one whose logic besets every plea for a "third way"—*neti neti, coincidentia oppositorum*, sublation, postcolonial ambivalence, polydoxical complexity. Every attempt to move beyond sheer opposition, two-party dualism, heterosexist exclusion, etc. seems to be threatened with collapse into the very terms we mean to alter in ourselves, to diffract, to queer, rather than to continue merely to mirror in reverse. But then in this house of mirrors—a capacious, cathedralesque one to be sure—it would be only *right* to unfold differently, not to supersede, the Christian tradition, which is already a manifold. In this we *certainly* oppose any oppositionalism that represses the doxically uncertain multiplicity of its own dogma. And so we claimed in our Introduction that polydoxy "does not fold orthodoxy down; it *complicates* it" (Keller and Schneider, "Introduction," 8). Ward responds: "then maybe orthodoxy is actually already more complicated than polydoxy gives it credit for." No doubt.

Yet, one might have read our volume as one long insistence upon the complication of orthodoxy. Many of us were at pains to acknowledge key moments of the complexification of orthodoxy—not in order to flatter the fathers but also not merely to rub their noses in their own disavowed multiplicities. We needed to crib certain theologoumena crucial to our own work. For instance, we made much of the complication the (orthodox) Christian trinity performs upon the biblical fidelity to and Hellenistic logic of the One. Schneider had already yoked her challenge to monotheism (that *modern* term) with the assertively orthodox and African emergence of trinitarian thinking in Tertullian.[3] And I had long ago linked the alternative logic of Tertullian's triune "different not separate" back to the Hebrew plurisingularity of Eloh*im* as an originative complication.[4] Mayra Rivera, as noted, writes her essay on *doxa* as a hermeneutic of John, the gospel more attractive to orthodoxy than the other three combined (Rivera, "Glory: the first passion of theology?"). Marion Grau lifts up the Anglican missionary Colensos, albeit dismissed as heretics for their respectful entanglement in Zulu culture (Grau, "Signs taken for polydoxy in a Zulu Kraal: creative friction manifested in missionary-native discourse," 217–237). For John Thatamanil, the "commitment to polydoxy finds expression in the theology of religious diversity" he is unfolding (Thatamanil, "God as ground, contingency, and relation: trinitarian polydoxy and religious diversity," 255). But that diversity is itself for him explicated in "a trinitarianism of ground, contingency, and relation"—for him rigorously articulable in terms of a classical Christian *perichoresis* (Thatamanil," "God as ground, contingency, and relation," 254). And precisely in its polydox orthodoxy, it funds the "collaborative conversation" of Christian comparative theology with specifically Hindu and Buddhist traditions (Thatamanil, "God as ground," 240). Mary-Jane Rubenstein finds in Augustine a precious breakthrough of "*profunda et infinita multiplicitas*," of multiplicity *as* his very self, mind, memory (Rubenstein, "Undone by each other: interrupted sovereignty in Augustine's *Confessions*," 105–125). That he defaults "to the unity from which we disintegrated into multiplicity" only intensifies her appreciation of the "polydox potential" at the "very heart of this monodox world" (Rubenstein, "Undone by each other," 123).

I could continue this processional march through this community of authors. But again it will begin to sound, misleadingly, like an apologetics. Even if monodoxy, not orthodoxy, is our opponent, we may not give orthodoxy the credit Ward considers its due. Even if we do not consider orthodoxy as such our Other or enemy, neither do we defend it—as such. We participate in the indefinite multiplicity of spiritual discourses and practices, many of them Christian; we witness to their vulnerable complexity in the face of aggressive competitors—of reactionary Christianity or reactive secularism. We may not realize that we have extra credit to give. We are so in debt to the variously orthodox traditions that fund us (often quite literally) that we may underestimate—at our own peril—their vulnerabilities and their promises.

At the same time, we owe the orthodoxies to which we are nonseparably related the gift of our differences. There is still too little in what defines itself as orthodox that has accepted experiments in theological complexity,

---

[3] Laurel Schneider, *Beyond Monotheism: A Theology of Multiplicity* (New York: Routledge, 2008), 53–73.

[4] Catherine Keller, *Face of the Deep: A Theology of Becoming* (New York: Routledge, 2003), 231.

religious multiplicity and apophatic becoming as intrinsically valuable—indeed as a gift. The exceptions remain marginal. For instance, if Nicholas of Cusa has a high notion of *complicatio*—a name for infinite divinity in which all is "folded together," not to be opposed to unity or to multiplicity but to "duality"—it hardly survived in subsequent theologies (except in Bruno, burnt as a heretic for it). He is one of the earliest Christian thinkers to routinely and respectfully name non-Christian others, not only Plato and Aquinas, but "pagans" with multiple deities, Maimonides and every then-known religion.[5] Cardinal Cusa surely presumed his orthodoxy and defended it against Wenck's attempt to expose him as a heretic. His thought, however, is not motivated by the defense and interpretation of known doctrine but by the adventure in "learned ignorance." Perhaps I make my own appeal to orthodoxy by summoning him. He represents one example of the ongoing process of a complexification that is avowedly open, even to religious others as sources of possible truth. But we think together here half a millennium later, and still tiptoe around the multiplicity of extra-Christian religious truths. Comparative theology, presupposing the multiplicity of religious truth, is now however advancing amidst thinkers such as Francis Clooney, who neither dilute nor oppose classical Christian confession. Thatamanil, building earlier upon a Tillichian and Advaitan sense of divine immanence, works with a notion of comparison rooted deeply within Christian doctrine.[6]

In other words, the gift of the polydoxical difference cannot be received without opening to yet more difference—that first of all of all those friends who do not thank us if we generously grant them anonymous Christian cover. So then I warm to Ward's reading of the Gospel of John's notion of friendship. "Friendship also allows for a variety of degrees of association, for the intensities, the collegialities, and the range of acquaintance that characterizes interrelationality; for no relation is the same and all the affective registers of relations are subject to change." Then, however, he adds: "There is again a multiplicity of possibilities of relation here but they are governed Christologically; they belong to and in Christ." One can squeeze such a sovereign abstraction out of John. But the spirit then differs from the offer—among friends—of the way, the water or the vine. When one asserts this gubernatorial belonging, most of the non-Christians I know (including the Jewish spouse) would feel kicked right out of the association. He (for example) will not understand his relations, even to his peculiarly Christian theologian partner, to be "governed Christologically." Yet he would have no problem with my reading of my relation to him as metaphorically "in Christ," nor as Christ as *one* name for the most loving of relations—depending upon the context and the care of the naming.

---

[5] Nicholas of Cusa, *De docta Ignorantia*, I.25 and I.26, and *De Pace Fidei*.
[6] John J. Thatamanil, *The Immanent Divine: God, Creation and the Human Predicament* (Minneapolis, MN: Fortress Press, 2006).

It is of course because Ward has with such care raised questions that we might in our polydoxical collective otherwise avoid that I linger with this particular dialogue. He is with reason concerned that a "simple panentheism," even possibly an "apophatic panentheism," realizes that God is "in all" but not that God "governs," and through a governance that would be supremely manifest in the full divinity of Christ. I do think actually there would be, even for a process theologian (which is, I note, not the same as a polydox one) some sense in which that governance can be expressed as a cosmic logos echoed in laws we cannot help but obey (gravity, or E=MC^2, or the uncertainty principle) and, in rougher than mathematical translation, in some we had best obey (the 10, the Golden Rule). But process or polydox panentheists would be so preoccupied to distinguish such governance from its routine associations with divine omnipotence and its echoes in every institution of coercive power; in fact it would be so cosmically and socially intent on democratizing the root figuration of "governance," that I suspect its "divine lure" may not appear to be governance at all.

If as Whitehead so memorably phrased it, "the Church gave unto God the attributes which belonged exclusively to Caesar,"[7] the Christocratic coins still in circulation are not made innocent by their antiquity. Of course I write in the context of the United States, with its formidable "capitalist Christian resonance machine" and not in Europe, with its gorgeously and harmlessly aging old stone churches. But they too have their ghosts. I fear that it is where Christ's governance is asserted that I cannot sense Christ governing; nor do I hear right teaching where orthodoxy is claimed. When "belonging to Christ" means that "we" and not "they" get the goods of salvation—I do not see the love. It may be that the deconstruction of classical omnipotence, a linchpin of process theology, makes possible a notion of divine efficacy, influence and not mere all-in-all immanence, that does not betray the love. The *law* of love: Do unto them as you would have them do unto you: . . . Respect the nonseparability of difference. The difference of another religion, enfolded in love, does not mean the equal validity of its "beliefs." No more can one validate as equal the truth-claims of all Christians who espouse more or less orthodox Christian beliefs. You might have an equal right to your belief, if you do not impose it on me; that does not mean that our beliefs are equally right. Nor do they carry equal weight in our respective communities.

Still, it is helpful to burrow for a moment into the soteriological core of "right belief," which *Polydoxy* may too earthily evade; or as Ward nails it, without which our Christianity becomes "ungrammatical": "the Christian promise, given through the resurrection of Christ, is that those who follow faithfully will be likewise resurrected." Though some of my co-authors

---

[7] Alfred North Whitehead, *Process and Reality: An Essay in Cosmology* (New York: Free Press, 1978/1985), 342.

might, I do not disagree with the proposition or with its promise—in it is encoded the distributive force of Easter. But I remain unmoved by much of what is likely to be heard by its terms. It readily stirs the egotism of salvation (will *I* get to live happily ever after?) and the misalignment of "faithfulness" with an omnipotently guided providential teleology confusing "promise" with "guarantee." Moreover, it routinely shifts attention to a supernatural, extracosmic salvation, sucking energy out of those worldly intercorporealities Ward certainly minds. And it rarely fails to mean that it is *Christians* who will be saved. The options Ward worries are left to us—a Hegelian becoming-God who needs saving, a local savior with mere pockets of "creative transformation," or multiple saviors fragmenting salvation history—would be worrisome indeed. But becomingness (a term coined by the great landscape architect Olmsted over a century ago) does not make one pathetic, but passionate; and a multiplicity of soteriological trajectories may now work to generate planetary solidarity as well as disintegration. Of course the long hegemony of Christian orthodoxy (with the whole sin/judgment/salvation apparatus) intensified fragmentation by attempting to squelch Christian, let alone religious, multiplicity. The imposition of its western grammar upon the polyglossal earth has at best advanced creative transformation in local pockets. At worst it has made the test of Christological pronunciation its deadly shibboleth—operative at any critical crossing and projected to final judgment. The ultimate drama of inclusive exclusion has driven theologians from Origen to Barth to the heresy of universal salvation. And a generous heresy it is, surely closer to a God who is love, and infinitely so.

If I imagine a polydox St. Peter at the pearly gates, he is saying: Oh dear, O dears. If you could barely love a few friends down there, well, welcome to heavenly love! Translation: If you are repelled *now* by this mottled multiplicity, with its needy, noisy, misguided human multitudes, let alone the inhuman reaches of animals, aliens and electrons, imagine what it will be like to be tangled up with them all in a God who is All in All. What for some would be heaven might be hell for you.

Polydoxically rendered, the trope of the resurrection does not occlude the multitude of vulnerable earthly bodies but re/members them, entwined together in glory. Life resurgent, life insurgent. Something like the roots and branches of the thrice annihilated, thrice reborn forest out her window, in Wendy Farley's achingly resurrective last metaphor: "To be beautiful, each being individually and each co-present with the other life forces of the forest, a song of mutuality." And, really, for Ward—as I think for this entire multiplicity of authors—the difference that counts when it comes to testing the viability of any pluralism seems not to lie with difference of religion, creed, or afterlife expectancy, so much as of ethical action in support of those vulnerable bodies human and otherwise. But, again, if polydoxy acquiesces in its pluralism, it is insufficient as a theory for such action. It may turn actually self-defeating, like the stupefied indecision of Buridan's ass. Or worse: "Multiplicity," writes Ward in his wrap up, naming what would be our direst sin, "embraces a multitude of sins and sinners and sinned against."

Indeed. As does the sun that shines on the righteous and the unrighteous alike. And just as the sun exposes self-righteousness, it gives the unrighteous no cover. So we cannot claim "to be perfect as the father is . . ." Finally the proof of any pluralism, which kicks it beyond relativism, will be its translation of the love of the enemy (Lord, even of our straightwhitemale theological foes.) Might we once and for all recognize the difference between a value-free relativism and value-loaded relationalism—in its strict analogy to that between separation and differentiation?

It is not my exteriority to another any more than my encapsulation of that other that energizes the planetary ethic we all want. It is a practicable mutuality that emerges as we find ourselves interdependent in our very otherness. In our sin-rich, *Han*-ridden, multitude. My sense of value—of what matters, and yes, of my own mattering, my value—surges not as mere difference and not as sheer unity. It makes itself felt, affectively, prehensively, in the pulsation of those mutualities bleeding off beyond kin and ken. There may be no consistent progress in history, there may be no defeat of entropy, but there are certainly dense braids of welcome evolution. They leave their traces when they fail. The Christian experiment in universal love, amidst its colossal failures, still collects into world-historical movements of nonviolence; it influences, often invisibly, forfeiting our triumphalist language of final guarantee, every network for gender, sexual, social and ecological justice. It may gather itself effectively in social movements, whose waves fall short but come again. Amidst our becoming. Whatever is coming.

If difference is relation, then what is becoming—what becomes us, what lends value and dignity and beauty—will be painfully selective. All things flow, but not anything goes. What Crockett dubs our "postmodern polyglossia" makes its "mani-folded choice" or "polyhairesis": it is not calling all, but many. It is calling those who may be capable of hearing the call, which is a promising call, a vocation to love the living, to live the loving. Perhaps too few will seem "chosen"—to the impossible love-embrace of a creepy, poisoned, still promising world. The promise of its future harmonies will surely enfold great polyphonies, symphonic dissonances. Ward concludes surprisingly, by donning the persona of Tolkien's Melkor, the dissonant one, vis-à-vis the ambiguous gift of polydoxy. Illuvatar works the music of dissonance into world-creation. Indeed Melkor, a fetchingly Luciferic dissident, is no polydox hero: it is his assistant, Sauron, who crafts the sheerest anti-multiplicity, archetype of Schneider's "logic of the One": "One ring to rule them all." Of course even Frodo was tempted to keep the ring. So polydoxy must surely confess to being tempted to the uniting power of orthodoxy old or new. But it is through what one commentator calls a "polydox effort" of dwarves, elves, wizards, eagles, hobbits, and even Gollum that the ring is finally destroyed.[8]

When oneness teaches and practices rightly, then it embraces multiplicity. The embrace melts the ring of power. Embrace is not enclosure. The circles of certainty—of whichever politics, of whichever beliefs—will of course form again, will again offer the counterfeit confidence. But the specifically apophatic twist of an ethical entanglement is perhaps just this: to insist that the margin of unknowing gives the difficult other the benefit of the doubt. Even or above all God—given His Death, given Her Rebirth, given the Dao and Chi of its Trinity[9] and the apophatic hope of a theology without cruelty and without cliché—offers us the benefit of our doubt. But then it is theology that benefits, when that of which Crockett concludes "you can call it God if you like" undoes the "Lord, Lord" business.

Still. The question remains acute, asked by more than one of the writers in this special issue, as to whether this isn't all, well, academic; just more self-indulgent, impotently good intention. Of course it is academics asking the question, of academics. Oh the circles. Surely Wendy Farley's challenge blesses this whole project: "The polydox, the fellow travelers, will put aside journals like this one, leave their libraries and computers and go into the world." We unsay ourselves not just into contemplative silence but into noisy action. Once and for all? Or in pulses, waves, spirals? At the same time and in that going forth, the work of theology, the work of theos in and as logos doesn't leave off, as Mark Jordan admonishes us all: "The arduous purpose of theological writing is luring readers into forms of speech that none of you has been taught to read, much less to speak." He suggests that it is in the communality of this writing that we learn "courage, the first passion of theological writing." If so, may the gifted dissonances and the unpredictable resonances of this very conversation encourage a multitude.

---

[8] Elijah Pruitt-Davis, e-mail message to author, May 9, 2013.

[9] Crockett is, here, riffing on Hyo-dong Lee's Daoist transliteration of the Christian trinity: "For lack of better words, I call it dao (source). I call it qi (energy). I call it shen (spirit). Here is an asymmetrical polydoxic trinitarian (un-)naming, in the mode of an English transliteration of Chinese, a sort of postmodern polyglossia.

INDEX

Modern Theology 2014
ISSN 0266-7177 (Print)
ISSN 1468-0025 (Online)

DOI: 10.1111/moth.12127

CONTRIBUTORS BIOS

Virginia Burrus is Bishop W. Earl Ledden Professor of Religion at Syracuse University. Her teaching and research interests in the field of ancient Christianity include gender, sexuality, and the body; martyrdom and asceticism; ancient novels and hagiography; constructions of orthodoxy and heresy; histories of theology and historical theologies. She is the author of *The Sex Lives of Saints: An Erotics of Late Ancient Hagiography* (2004), *Saving Shame: Martyrs, Saints, and Other Abject Subjects* (2007), and (with Mark Jordan and Karmen MacKendrick) *Seducing Augustine: Desire, Bodies, Confessions* (2010). She is past President of the North American Patristics Society, Associate Editor of the *Journal of Early Christian Studies*, and co-editor of the University of Pennsylvania Press series "Divinations: Rereading Late Ancient Religion."

Shannon Craigo-Snell is Professor of Theology at Louisville Presbyterian Theological Seminary. Her constructive work draws upon systematic theology, feminist theory, and performance studies. She is the author of two books: *Silence, Love, and Death: Saying "Yes" to God in the Theology of Karl Rahner* (2008) and *Living Christianity: A Pastoral Theology for Today* (coauthored with Shawnthea Monroe, 2009). Her most recent book, *The Empty Church: Theatre, Theology, and Hope*, is forthcoming with Oxford University Press.

Clayton Crockett is Associate Professor and Director of Religious Studies at the University of Central Arkansas. He is the author or co-author of five books, most recently *Deleuze Beyond Badiou: Ontology, Multiplicity, and Event* (2013). He is a co-editor, along with Slavoj Zizek, Creston Davis and Jeffrey W. Robbins, of the book series "Insurrections: Critical Studies of Religion, Politics and Culture" for Columbia University Press.

Wendy Farley is Professor of Theology and Ethics at Emory University. Her research is rooted in philosophical theology and, more recently, contemplative and comparative theology. She has written several books on these topics, including *The Wounding and Healing of Desire: Weaving Heaven and Earth* (2005), *Eros for the Other: Retaining Truth in a Pluralistic World* (2006), and *Gathering Those Driven Away: A Theology of Incarnation* (2011).

Mark D. Jordan teaches in the Danforth Center on Religion and Politics at Washington University in St. Louis. His most recent book is *Recruiting Young Love: How Christians Talk about Homosexuality* (University of Chicago Press 2011). His next book, to be published by Stanford in 2014, will treat Foucault, religion, and mute resistance in bodies.

Catherine Keller is Professor of Constructive Theology in the Graduate Division of Religion at Drew University. She has authored several books, including *Apocalypse Now and Then* (Augsburg, 1996), *Face of the Deep: A Theology of Becoming* (Routledge, 2003), and *On the Mystery* (Fortress, 2008). She has co-edited many works besides *Polydoxy*, including several others in the Transdisciplinary Theological Colloquia Series (Fordham). Currently she is completing *The Cloud of the Impossible: Theological Entanglements.*

Mary-Jane Rubenstein is Associate Professor of Religion at Wesleyan University. Her research and teaching are focused in continental philosophy of religion, philosophy and history of science, and gender and sexuality studies. She is the author of *Strange Wonder: The Closure of Metaphysics and the Opening of Awe* (2009) and of *Worlds without End: The Many Lives of the Multiverse* (2014).

Laurel C. Schneider, recently appointed Professor of Religious Studies at Vanderbilt University, was Professor of Theology, Ethics, and Culture at Chicago Theological Seminary from 1999-2013. She is the author of *Beyond Monotheism* (2007) and *Re-Imagining the Divine* (1998), in addition to co-editing *Polydoxy* with Catherine Keller. She is co-chair of the national Workgroup in Constructive Theology, and has written numerous articles at the intersections of feminism, theology, queer theory, poetics, Native American studies, and postcolonial theory.

Kathryn Tanner is Frederick Marquand Professor of Systematic Theology at Yale Divinity School. She is the author of *Theories of Culture: A New Agenda for Theology* (Fortress, 1997) and *Economy of Grace* (Fortress, 2005), among other books.

Linn Marie Tonstad is assistant professor of systematic theology at Yale Divinity School. She is currently completing her first book, tentatively titled *God and Difference: Experimental Trinitarian Theology.*

Graham Ward is the Regius Professor of Divinity at the University of Oxford and former Head of the School of Arts, Histories and Cultures at the University of Manchester. Among his books are *Cities of God* (2002), *Cultural Transformation and Religious Practice* (2005), *True Religion* (2003), *Christ and Culture* (2005) and *The Politics of Discipleship* (2009). His next book, *Unbelievable*, will be published by I. B. Taurus in 2013.